Welcome!

The Fellowship for Intentional Community is pleased to offer you the cream of our crop—the very best articles that have appeared over the last 20 years in our flagship publications: *Communities* magazine and *Communities Directory*. We've distilled what we consider the most insightful and helpful articles on the topics that you—our readers—have told us you care about most, and have organized them into 15 scintillating collections:

I. Intentional Community Overview; Starting a Community
II. Seeking and Visiting a Community
III. Leadership, Power, and Membership
IV. Good Meetings
V. Consensus

VI. Agreements, Conflict, and Communication
VII. Relationships, Intimacy, Health, and Well-Being
VIII. Children in Community
IX. Community for Elders
X. Sustainable Food, Energy, and Transportation
XI. Green Building, Ecovillage Design, and Land Preservation
XII. Cohousing
XIII. Cooperative Economics and Creating Community Where You Are
XIV. Challenges and Lessons of Community
XV. The Peripatetic Communitarian: The Best of Geoph Kozeny

On average, each collection is comprised of 15–20 articles, containing a total of 55–65 pages. All are available both as downloadable PDFs and as print copies. Buy one, buy several, or buy the whole set! While there's a smattering of classic pieces that date back to the '90s, the vast majority of these offerings have been written in the past dozen years, representing cutting-edge thinking and how-to explorations of the social, ecological, and economic aspects of sustainable living. We've gathered insights about what you can expect when raising children in community, and offer a wealth of information about what it's like to grow old there, too. For dessert, we have the collected wisdom of over 50 essays from Geoph Kozeny (1949–2007), the Peripatetic Communitarian.

If you're hungry for information about cooperative living, we have a menu that will satisfy any appetite! If you're thinking about starting a community, this collection offers an incredible storehouse of practical advice. If you're thinking of joining a community, our packets will help you discern the right things to look for, and how to be a savvy shopper. If you're just curious about community and want to snack, our smörgåsbord of tasty nuggets will let you pick and choose what's most appealing.

Bon appétit!

Laird Schaub
FIC Executive Secretary
November 2013

Seeking and Visiting a Community

If you're seriously interested in community living, all experts agree that you're wise to visit first. Not just because reality may not align exactly with the mental image you had based on written descriptions or phone calls, but because what you *think* you want and what you *actually* want aren't necessarily the same thing, and it's far cheaper to discover that *before* you sell your home and move to another zip code.

These 14 articles address how to get the most out of community visits, and also share diverse stories of community exploration. They walk you through the etiquette of setting up a visit (hint: don't drop in unannounced), how to put your hosts at ease, and how to ask the right questions. They also provide tips to communities themselves on how to deal optimally with community-seekers.

—Laird Schaub. FIC Executive Secretary, November 2013

Red Carpets and Slammed Doors

Visiting Communities

by Geoph Kozeny

Hoping to visit a community? The good news is that most communities welcome visitors, and a majority of those are open to new members. The bad news? Because so many community seekers want to visit, many communities at some point experience visitor overload and feel burned out from the seemingly never-ending flow of strangers. The best news: if you're considerate and persistent, the odds are good that you'll be able to arrange a visit and have a great experience.

An essential element of planning a satisfying visit is getting really clear about exactly what you want from a community. In other words, what is the purpose of your visit? You'll save considerable time and effort if you can learn to intuit how well any given community's reality will match with the picture you've envisioned. There's definitely an art to this prescreening process, as it's based solely on information from written materials, letters, phone calls, emails, and perhaps a website—nothing physical that you can actually see, touch, smell, or taste.

While you're exploring communities from a distance, it also pays to sort through, point by point, all the different characteristics you think you want. Ask yourself: which attributes are mandatory, which are strong preferences, and which are nice but not necessary? This *Directory* is probably the best resource you'll find to aid in wrapping your mind around the possibilities. Carefully study each group's entry in the cross-reference chart and its written description in the listings section. With practice you can learn to use that information to spot potential incompatibilities in visions, values, and social norms. And please, don't assume that the community welcomes visitors just because they're listed in this book. Be sure to check out the "Visitors Accepted" column in the charts.

Even under stress, many overloaded communities will agree to host more visitors, usually due to a sense of mission or obligation, but beware: often it is only the visitor coordinators and a few others who are enthusiastic about the idea. Some community members, typically acting from instinct rather than clarity, will go about their daily lives while keeping a low profile and acting distant in a weary, mostly subconscious attempt to minimize interactions with the newest batch of "tourists"—which might turn out to be you. Try not to take it personally.

Introductions and First Impressions

Usually the best line of first contact is through a friend who knows the community and is willing to give you a personal referral. If you don't have a friend with direct connections, friends-of-friends can prove just as effective.

Use your network of friends and acquaintances creatively. Let it be known that you're interested in visiting certain communities, and ask your friends if they—or anyone they know—has a connection to those groups. If through correspondence, or especially through a visit, you make a connection with a member of one community, ask that person if they can recommend an especially good contact at the other communities you hope to visit. If your feelers yield a connection, be sure to open your introductory letter or phone call by saying "So-and-so over at Community X referred you to me." On the other hand, avoid giving the impression that you're a name-dropper, or that you're trying to do an end-run around their official channels. Alienating the community's designated visitor coordinator is far from being the optimal way to start a visit.

If no leads materialize, there's still a reasonably good chance of making a fruitful connection through self-introduction. Avoid sending an email or letter that poses a long list of questions about the community, but provides little or no information about who you are and what you're seeking. Although there's a wide range of styles that can work well in a letter of inquiry, a good general formula is to give approximately equal emphasis to: (1) describing what you're looking for, how you heard about them, and why they interest you; (2) telling about your history, skills, and special needs; and (3) posing questions about their community and their visiting protocols.

Your letter should be short, to the point, and engaging—if you send a long letter, you run the risk of overwhelming them right off the bat, or of having your letter shunted to the needs-to-be-answered-but-requires-a-lot-of-time-and-energy-to-deal-with pile. Such letters, unfortunately, only occasionally make it back to the top of the priority pile. Usually a one-page letter (or the equivalent in email) is best, and two pages should be the absolute maximum—anything longer than that reduces your chances of getting a prompt response. If you want to be remembered, enclose a photo, artwork, doodles, an interesting article, or something else eye-catching to make your letter stand out in the crowd (but please—no confetti, glitter, or other mess-making surprises). And, if you are sending a paper letter, be sure to include a self-addressed stamped envelope (SASE).

You may also want to consider first visiting one or more groups located in your region. Even if they are not likely candidates for where you'll finally want to settle, you can hone your visitor skills. The fact that they're relatively easy to get to means you can get some visiting experience under your belt without a large investment of your time or resources. It can be pretty devastating to use up all your precious vacation traveling cross-continent to visit your dream community, only to discover that it's not at all what you had in mind (which is fairly common, by the way). Instead, go through the steps face-to-face with real people, and get comfortable doing the interviews, the work, and the socializing.

Following Up

The sad truth is that many groups don't respond to correspondence in a timely fashion, in spite of good intentions. The reality is that living in community can be very demanding—there's always so much to be done—and answering a stack of correspondence doesn't usually rank as high on the chore list as milking the cows, supervising the kids, taking out the recycling, or building the new community center.

If your letter or email has received no response after two to four weeks, try a follow up. If you still receive no response a short phone call is probably in order. Try to pick a time when folks are likely to be around and not otherwise busy. Often early evenings, or right before or after a meal, are good times to call. If you reach an answering machine, identify yourself, leave your number, and ask them to call you back at their convenience. Suggest times when you're most reachable, and explain that when they do get through, you'll be happy to hang up and call them right back on your dime.

When you reach a live person, first introduce yourself—mentioning your referral if you have one—and explain that you're interested in visiting. Be sure to note that you've already sent a letter. Ask whoever answers if he or she is a good person to talk with about visiting and arrangements, and verify that this is a good time to talk. If the time's not right, make a date to call back at a better time. If they suggest you talk with someone else, note the new name, and ask for suggestions about how and when to reach the identified contact person. When you do finally connect with your contact person, be sure to verify up-front all the details related to visiting (see sidebar on p. 27).

If you wrote and got no response, it's usually far better to call first rather than show up unannounced. However, if they have no phone listing in the *Directory*, if their line's always busy, or if their published number has been disconnected and the community has no listing in Directory Assistance, then an exploratory "Hello" might be in order. If you've tried well in advance to reach a community but received no reply, it may work to "drop by" for a few minutes to introduce yourself—but be sensitive to their energy levels. Be prepared to find accommodations elsewhere, and arrange to come back when it's convenient for them. A 10- or 15-minute visit may be all that's appropriate if you catch them in the middle of something—but if your timing's good, you might get the deluxe two-hour tour right on the spot, plus get invited to dinner. Be flexible.

Drop-in visitors can be especially awkward for groups that are far off the beaten path, but in most cases you can locate a park or a campground within commuting distance. If they remember your letter, they'll know you made a bona fide effort to set up a visit and that they were the ones to drop the ball by not responding—so make your letter memorable.

Always remember: the community you want to visit is also somebody's home...

Fitting In

Always remember: the community you want to visit is also somebody's home, so plan on using the same standards you would use if visiting a hometown friend or relatives you see only occasionally.

Often it's helpful to figure out why they're open to visitors in the first place. They may be: seeking new members, needing help with the work, wanting the stimulation of meeting new people, and/or spreading their vision (e.g., egalitarianism, ecovillages) or religion (including the promotion of "community").

What will they gain from your stay? There are infinite ways to plug in and make yourself useful. Pitch in with everyday chores such as gardening, farm work, construction projects, bulk mailings, cooking, cleaning, dishes, or childcare. You may gain "Much Appreciated Guest" status if you have special skills to offer: layout or graphic design (newsletters), computer skills, meeting facilitation, storytelling, music, or massage. One fellow I met is a chiropractor who plies his trade for free at each community he visits. A woman therapist offers private and group counseling sessions to community members. Another fellow built a solar oven at each community he visited. Alternative building technologies, permaculture, and composting toilet expertise are all skills generally in high demand. Often, however, the most appreciated contribution is your willingness to pitch in to help with whatever boring chore needs doing at the moment.

Often, however, the most appreciated contribution is your willingness to pitch in to help with whatever boring chore needs doing at the moment.

Some groups are not organized in a way that lets them take advantage of visitor labor, and your desire to pitch in can actually become more of a headache for them than a help. Use your intuition in such situations. Make suggestions, but be open—offer, but don't push too hard. If they aren't able to involve you in the work and don't have much time to spend with you, be prepared to entertain yourself: bring books, tapes, musical instruments, etc.

Some groups use a buddy system for orienting visitors, pairing each visitor with a community member who can serve as a guide and a liaison. Having an identified support person to turn to is often helpful. If the community you are visiting doesn't use such a system, you might look around for someone willing to fill that role.

It's important to be clear about your underlying motives so that both your expectations and the community's are realistic. Are you seeking a community to join, or gathering ideas about how groups deal with various issues so you can start your own? Perhaps you are just curious about shared living options and open to being inspired. Perhaps you're looking for a love affair or relationship. That may, in fact, be a possibility, but usually you'll alienate community members who sense you're on the prowl for romance rather than looking for community. What you're most likely to get in those situations is the hot seat, the cold shoulder, an invitation to leave, or some unpleasant combination of the three.

Sometimes awkward situations will come up, and it can take fairly sophisticated interpersonal skills to set things straight with your hosts. After all, many people have been conditioned to be stoic, and your hosts may be reluctant to say anything "impolite" about something you're doing that's bothering them. In those cases it's up to you to initiate the process of exploring any concerns or annoyances that they're sitting on, and it's much

Albert Bates – The Farm

"What will they gain from your stay? There are infinite ways to plug in and make yourself useful. Pitch in with everyday chores such as gardening, farm work, construction projects, bulk mailings, cooking, cleaning, dishes, or childcare."

better to get those things out in the open early in your visit, before unexpressed resentments fester. Gracefully facing awkward issues head-on will give you the option to work on them and to develop a rapport with your hosts. Ignoring the tension will usually feed the sense of alienation or mistrust, and prompt your hosts to close up a bit more with every interaction.

It's a warm and wonderful feeling to be included by the group and to experience a sense of "being in community" during your first visit, but don't count on it. Deep connections often take time, and sometimes come only after mutual trust and friendship have been solidly established.

Deep connections often take time, and sometimes come only after mutual trust and friendship have been solidly established.

Beyond First Impressions

"Being human" implies that we all bring along some baggage from our conditioning, and that we are seldom capable of living up to our own high standards. The discrepancy between our visions of an ideal world and the reality of our daily lives is probably the most common catalyst underlying the creation of new intentional communities. As a result, what we say we're going to do, both as individuals and as communities, is usually a lot more grandiose than what we actually accomplish. Keeping that perspective in mind while visiting communities can help keep your expectations in line with probabilities, and may ultimately help you avoid setting yourself up for a lot of unnecessary disappointment.

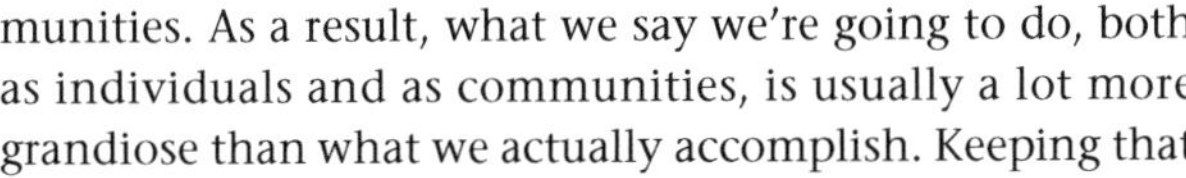

Visiting communities is much like dating—people have a tendency to put their best foot forward and try to hide what they consider to be weaknesses. It's helpful to fine-tune your eyes and ears to pick up pieces of the hidden story, and to sensitize yourself to what kinds of conversations and interactions will give you an accurate sense of the underlying day-to-day realities. Remember, undesirable habits are easily obscured when members are on their best behavior. If you visit at least a handful of communities, you can compare and contrast their strengths and weaknesses. There's no better way than visiting to learn what to look for and where to find it.

Resources For Starting Your Own Community

One of the best ways to prepare yourself to start your own community is to learn about communities that already exist, especially ones similar to what you would like to create. What do they look and feel like? How are they organized? How do they make decisions? How do they own their property?

One way to answer these questions is by in-person visits, of course, and this *Communities Directory* can help you find and contact them. Each community you visit will give you ideas about what you do and don't want in your own community. You can also—if you're polite and respectful of people's time—ask questions. How did the founders start up the community? What are they really glad they did? Do they recommend that you do the same? On the other hand, what do they wish they'd never done and suggest you not do?

Another way to "visit" communities is to watch Geoph Kozeny's *Visions of Utopia* video documentary, parts one and two (available at *store.ic.org*). Each video profiles a wide range of communities—from urban group households to rural ecovillages, service-oriented communities, spiritual communities, and cohousing neighborhoods. You'll get a lot of good ideas from listening to members of these communities give their opinions on a variety of topics.

Browsing the Internet is also a good way to learn about communities. Look for community vision and purpose statements, community goals, visitor policies, documents and bylaws. You can get great ideas about your forming community's agreements and policies just by reading what hundreds of communities are happy to share publicly on their own websites. The FIC's websites at *www.ic.org* and *directory.ic.org* are great places to start, but you can also see the list of Networks of Intentional Communities (p. 20) for more websites.

Reading stories about how different communities have faced and resolved challenges is another excellent way to prepare. Of course, we recommend the FIC's quarterly *Communities* magazine, where you'll find articles on ecovillages, cohousing neighborhoods, as well as rural, urban, income-sharing, and spiritual communities. Among other topics, there are often special articles on communication and process skills, membership issues, and sustainability projects. For sample issues, back issues, and subscriptions visit *store.ic.org*. Read about starting up and living in cohousing communities in *Cohousing* magazine, online at *www.cohousing.org/magazine*.

To dig deeper, learn how to ask friendly but penetrating questions. After you've gotten to know a new group well enough to get more personal, try posing such open-ended queries as:

- What are some of the things you like best about living here? The least?
- What's the most difficult issue your community has had to deal with in the last year, or in the last five years?
- How many members have left in the past year or two, and why did they leave?
- How has the community changed over the years? What changes would you like to see in the future?
- What are some of the big challenges your community is facing now?
- How has living here contributed to your personal growth and happiness?

If the community members perceive you as being sincere, interested, and open-minded, most will be willing to engage with you in a thoughtful dialogue. However, if they sense that you've already made up your mind about what's right—and are likely to pass judgment on them—not much information will be forthcoming.

> The best way to learn about yourself, and about the communities themselves, is to visit.

Avoid stereotypes of how you think communities should be. If you assume they will have any particular standard or feature you associate with "communities"—things like art facilities, organic gardens, health food, homeschooling, sexual openness—you're asking for disappointment. Many will have at least a few of those features, but few will have them all. Being outspoken or opinionated about the "shoulds" is an easy way to wear out your welcome fast—or to not get invited in the first place, if it shows up during the introductory phase. If something you value highly seems to be missing, ask them about it. Would they be open to it in the future? Would there be room and support for you to introduce it? Present your concern as, "Is it likely the group would be open to this?" rather than, "I couldn't live here unless."

While probing for deeper understanding, be sensitive to members' needs for privacy and quiet time, and to what kind of energy you're putting out. If you make a good personal connection, chances are good that they'll be happy to offer you hospitality. Otherwise, hosting you tends to become a chore for them, or worse, an annoyance.

The FIC also hosts one- or two-day-long Art of Community gatherings in various regions of North America. You can take workshops by some of the most experienced community founders and veterans in the Communities Movement, and meet like-minded souls from your region. You might discover co-creators for your own community project sitting across from you at lunch. Other organizations also host communities conferences and workshops on community. For schedules and more information see our online events calendar at *www.ic.org/events*.

When you want to get down to the nuts and bolts of starting a new community, we recommend *Creating a Life Together: Practical Tools to Grow Ecovillages and Intentional Communities*, written by *Communities* magazine editor Diana Leafe Christian (New Society Publishers, 2003). Diana spent years learning everything she could from community founders about what does and doesn't work when starting a new community. Chapters cover typical timeframes and costs, characteristics of community founders, tips on getting started as a group, crafting vision and purpose documents, decision making and governance, finding and financing land, neighbors and zoning, legal structures, site planning, communication and process, and selecting new people.

You can also gain valuable information by reading a how-we-did-it story by community founder Liz Walker in *EcoVillage At Ithaca: Pioneering a Sustainable Culture* (New Society Publishers, 2005). Liz takes you step by step through the joys and challenges of the community-building process—the firsthand experience of folks who did it, and did it successfully. EcoVillage at Ithaca is both an ecovillage and two clustered cohousing communities, so you'll learn about the start-up issues of both kinds of projects.

Another helpful guide is *The Cohousing Handbook, Second Edition*, by Chris and Kelly ScottHanson (New Society Publishers, 2004). It contains information that would benefit people starting non-cohousing, as well as cohousing, communities. Areas of focus include: forming the core group, buying land, the design process, legal issues, finance and budget, and marketing and membership.

For more ideas on cohousing communities, see *Cohousing: A Contemporary Approach to Housing Ourselves, Second Edition*, by Kathryn McCamant, Charles Durrett, and Ellen Hertzman (Ten Speed Press, 1994). If you are specifically interested in community design, see *Rebuilding Community in America*, by Ken Norwood and Kathleen Smith (Shared Living Resource Center, 1995). All books are available from the FIC's Community Bookshelf at *store.ic.org*.

What's Really Important?

Having talked to thousands of community seekers over several decades, I am convinced that most of us do not truly know what would make us happy, nor do we see how habits we've developed over the decades stand in the way of our accomplishing the things we say we want. It's only after we've tried something a time or two that we really understand how important, or not, that thing is to our happiness. For example, I've witnessed dozens of back-to-the-land dreamers who moved to the country to do gardening, raise livestock, chop wood, and carry water—only to discover that those things are hard work that cause calluses, sunburn, mosquito bites, sore backs, and are subject to the harsh unpredictabilities of nature. Many of those dreamers adapt to the reality and subsequently thrive in that environment, but nearly as many decide to move back to a more urban, less physically demanding lifestyle.

Real-life experience can be similarly eye-opening for folks with visions of a community based on shared ownership, cooperative businesses, and consensus decision making. Living that way can certainly be inspiring and fulfilling, but because most of us have grown up in a society that emphasizes individualism and competition, we are often surprised by how challenging and frustrating the cooperative life can be. Often we fail to see how our attitudes and actions are contributing to the problems rather than generating solutions.

Living in intentional community is a lot of hard work, but it's a noble undertaking that offers great rewards for those with enough vision and perseverance to stick with it.

One problem stems from the fact that we conduct mostly mental research and don't get nearly enough hands-on experience. The best way to learn about yourself, and about the communities themselves, is to visit. In that context you can experiment with balancing work involvement with social involvement, and experience how easy (or not!) it is for you to adapt to a new culture.

Love at First Sight?

Investigating communities that are based on the idea of creating a better life can be very refreshing. However, be warned: there is a tendency to fall in love with the first group visited. It usually pays to check out a few more anyway. Your first impression may be based on the excitement of discovering the many ways the group's vision matches your own, but be sure that you also look for the differences. For a good match, both you and the community need to be able to tolerate each other's rough edges.

There may have been some common interactions that you missed. Did you get to see the group go through a meeting process? Did you watch them deal with a challenging issue? People's rough edges are most likely to show up when they're under heavy stress, so unless you saw them under pressure, you'll probably leave with an incomplete picture of how well they fare when dealing with interpersonal tensions. If you do witness them working on a conflict, try to hear both sides and watch to see if they approach differences with an open mind.

If you develop closeness with folks in one subgroup, you will most likely see and hear an incomplete picture of the issues and norms in question. Seek out members holding an opposing point of view, and see if you can understand their side of the issue. It's also possible that a few influential members are away, and the vibe at the community may be very different when they're home—more supportive if it's a primary nurturer/diplomat who's absent, or more strained if it's the chief skeptic/troublemaker who's gone. Additionally, there may be other visitors present whose issues or energy affect the dynamics.

You can learn a lot from other visitors, and from folks living in other communities. Both groups have a perspective that's somewhat detached from the hubbub of the everyday reality, and it's quite possible that they've witnessed the group under stress. Ex-members are also a great source of perspective on what tensions might be lurking below the surface, and how deep they're submerged.

It's usually a good idea to let your first impressions percolate before deciding to make a commitment to join a community. After a first visit, spend some time away from the group to see how well your initial impression holds up when you're no longer being influenced by their energy and enthusiasm. It's especially interesting and informative to listen to yourself handle questions about the community posed by your pre-community friends and acquaintances.

A Never-Ending Quest

No two communities are identical and, in fact, no community is the same today as it was five years ago—nor will it be the same five years hence. Visions change, priorities change, the cast of characters change, people get older, the weather gets colder. This ever-evolving nature makes the search for a community to join both interesting and challenging. What you experience during a first visit is unlikely to remain static, yet you must decide based on that initial impression. And you must be prepared to adapt to the shifts in values and priorities that will inevitably come with the passage of time.

With that in mind, pay careful attention to the ideas and interactions that feel best to you, noting whether it's the philosophy, the lifestyle, the place, or the people that touch you at the deepest level. If you feel yourself drawn most energetically to a group whose stated philosophy isn't very well aligned with your own, it will probably not work out for you to be there for the long haul. However, if they're open to it, consider spending more time with them in order to explore what makes it work for you on the energetic level. Similarly, for a community with ideals matching yours but a shortage of group chemistry, try spending enough time with them to learn about what's either lacking or overdone—what's getting in the way of the synergy?

Sorting through all the complexities can be overwhelming, and the best thing you can do to gain perspective and solace is to connect with others who can relate to what you're going through. If you know of friends who are also on a community quest, consider creating a support group to share experiences, insights, and leads. Scan the ads in the alternative press and on the bulletin boards of nearby co-ops and health food stores, looking for announcements of support groups and networking opportunities. Check out the Intentional Communities Web site, *www.ic.org*, and follow the links from there. Or participate in one of the FIC's community conferences, a veritable cornucopia of seekers, networkers, and communitarians coming together to share information on the hows, whys, and wheres of shared living. It's a special opportunity to learn a lot in a few days about a number of communities from a wealth of experienced communitarians, all in an atmosphere of community.

> It's usually a good idea to let your first impressions percolate before deciding to make a commitment to join a community.

Living in intentional community is a lot of hard work, but it's a noble undertaking that offers great rewards for those with enough vision and perseverance to stick with it. The first step in that process is finding a group compatible with your vision of a better world, and the rest of the work—for the rest of your life—will require an open mind, creativity, flexibility, commitment, integrity, common sense, and a lot of heart. Daunting? Yes, but worth it.

Get Things Clear Up Front

- Confirm that the community allows visitors, and that you'll be welcome to visit.
- Do they have particular times when visitors are welcome, regular visitor days, or a visitor program? Plan to be flexible to accommodate their scheduling needs.
- Do they have written Visitors' Guidelines that they could send you? Do they have policies or agreements about smoking, drugs, alcohol, diet, kids, pets, nudity, celibacy, quiet hours, etc. that you need to know about in advance? Usually it's best to leave pets at home.
- Do they have any literature about themselves that you can read in the meantime? Brochures? Copies of articles written about them? A website?
- Are there any costs involved (visitor fees, utilities, food)?
- Verify length of stay, and any work that will be expected of you. If no work is expected, ask if you'll be able to help them with their work projects. (This is one of the best ways to get to know individual members as well as to learn about the community's daily life.)
- Confirm what you will need to bring: bedding, towels, shampoo, rain gear, work clothes and gloves, special foods, etc. Inform them of any unusual needs you may have (diet, allergies, medications). To the extent possible, plan to cover for yourself so that meeting your special needs doesn't become a burden on the community.
- Let them know if you can provide your own accommodation, such as a tent, RV, or a van to sleep in. Sometimes, if they're feeling overwhelmed with visitors, being self-sufficient in that way will increase your chances of getting invited.
- If you are traveling by public transportation and need to be picked up, try to arrange a convenient time and place of arrival. If a special trip is required to pick you up, reimburse the community for their travel costs.
- Even if a community requires no visitor fees, offer to pitch in a few bucks for food and utility costs. Especially when visiting small communities, I like to bring a special treat for the members—a bag of fruit, almonds, gourmet coffee, ice cream (or non-dairy desserts for the vegans).
- If you need to alter your dates or cancel the visit, please inform the community immediately. They may have turned away other visitors in order to make room for you.

BY JULIE PENNINGTON

Visiting Communities: Tips for Guests and Hosts

On the second night of my visit to an intentional community, I lay shivering in my soggy tent making plans for revenge. It was the second day of thunderstorms, and my precious few still-dry clothes were piled inside my sleeping bag for preservation. The water supply had been out at the campsite where I was sleeping for my entire stay, and the rain dripping through my tent roof was no substitute for a real shower. All I wanted in the whole world was running water and a roof. This was not at all what I thought my long-awaited community visit would be like. My damp skin, dirty feet, and angry attitude came together to transform me from the smiling guest I had been at arrival to the bitter pouting one I'd become.

In the months preceding the visit I wrote letters, emailed, and spoke on the phone with my future hosts. Because of time restraints on my part, I could not stay for the regular guest period, and the community worked with my requests and allowed me to come outside of the normal visitor program. I was grateful and asked the necessary questions to ensure that all my ducks were in a row for the visit to go over smoothly. I brought as gifts homemade jam and blankets that I had crocheted myself, and wrote checks to more than cover my expenses. When I arrived I took care to respect the members' busy lives and thanked them for every conversation and meal. I wanted to do my part to be a "good guest," one whom community members would be glad to have as a new member. I was so intent on my role as a guest that I acted nervous and awkward and walked on eggshells to not disrupt their normal routines.

By day three of my damp and soggy predicament, still wearing my moldy dress and tangled hair, I was pretty sure I'd get no invitation to shower in someone's home or sleep on someone's floor. I knew that I had to stop walking on eggshells around these people and take responsibility for my own needs. I mentioned to leaders in the community, my host, and any other sympathetic ear that I was sleeping in the lightning with no water. But complaining that your neck hurts doesn't always get you a full-body massage. A few community members lamented my situation but did not offer any assistance, and I began to resent their clean clothes and well-rested spirits. I was feeling sorry for myself, and I was getting grouchier with each falling raindrop.

Why didn't I insist on what I needed? Advocate for myself more directly? I felt indebted to the group for their flexibility and assumed that I would have been pushing it to ask for anything more than the joy of their company and a place for my tent. This was when I threw my good-visitor hat into the plastic bag with the rest of my soaked belongings and became angry. I felt that if the community really wanted me to be there, they should take responsibility to pick up on my needs.

I spent the rest of my visit bitter and pouty.

Whether you live in a co-op, an ecovillage, an income-sharing commune, or any other type of intentional community, the best way to gain new members is through hosting visitors. It's an essential tool for furthering the communities movement and spreading the good word about community living, but it nevertheless is a task. I have come to believe that a good visiting experience is a two-way street. Both visitor and host must make commitments to one another for a short period, and there are things that each can do to make the time pleasant and productive.

Keep your objectives in mind and don't hesitate to ask for what you need.

As a guest, you can certainly take steps to get the most out of your experience. Set aside enough time for your stay to really get a feel for the community you are considering joining. Write a letter beforehand introducing yourself. Learn as much about the community as possible before the visit. Come prepared with questions and a good idea of what you're looking for. A piece of advice I've clung to during my visits to communities is "asking to ask." Remember that the community is not a tourist spot, but a home (and sometimes a workplace) to its members. Before ambushing residents with questions over their morning granola, it is a good idea to ease into conversation about the community by saying something like, "May I ask you a question?" By doing so, you give the member an opportunity to decline if she is busy or not in the mood to act as community spokesperson. Take the time to read other articles about how to visit communities (such as Geoph Kozeny's "Red Carpets and Slammed Doors" in the 2000 edition of the *Communities Directory*) or just ask experienced members for tips before you plan your trip.

Properly hosting a guest in a community takes a little more time and energy than simply showing the visitor where to eat and sleep. So what can we do as hosts to make the visitor's experience a good one? A structured visitor program sends the message to potential members that the community is well organized and cares about its guests.

A community should first decide what its position on visitors will be. What times visitors will be welcome, how long a visit can be, how many visitors you can host at a time, whether you can accommodate children, whether you can—or want to—accommodate pets, etc. Will there be one person or a team devoted to guests? What responsibility does the average member have to interact with the guest and tend to her or his needs?

It's a good idea for your group to draft a general letter about what to expect as a visitor in your community. Also, you might want to photocopy or reference an article about how to visit communities and send it to visitors ahead of time. A visitor liaison person or visitor team should be available to the visitors before their arrival to answer any questions and should inform other members of upcoming visits. Once the guests have arrived, the liaison person can make them feel welcome by introducing them to other community members. Suggest which members they can ask about various aspects of the community. Point out which members are in charge of labor, food, and finances, and which are long-time, experienced members, as compared to relatively newer members. Every community member has a special perspective on their community life, and visitors can make most efficient use of their time if they know whom to ask which kinds of questions. If you choose to do this, though, remember to ask the members' permission first for their various areas of expertise.

I've mentioned some steps you can take as a visitor before arriving at a community. But, as my soggy tale illustrates, good preparation may not grant you good-visitor status for your actual stay. What I learned from my visits this summer was the simple virtue of honesty. I was thrilled to be at the community I had dreamed about visiting for years, but my assumption that community members could read my mind put a damper on the trip. I am sure that members would have been eager to help had they only known what I needed.

Visitor periods are generally too short to learn every detail of community life, so it is to your advantage to make the most of your time spent there. If you consider the tips above before your trip, you'll be off to a good start. When you arrive, keep your objectives in mind and don't hesitate to ask for what you need. An attitude like I had could prevent you from getting what you came to experience. Keeping a journal of your stay is a great tool to help when you return home and consider membership in that particular community. You are there to gather information and check out the vibe of the group and the land. Keep your contact information of particularly helpful members, since more questions will probably arise after you leave and reflect on the experience. Remember your criteria for the community you'd like to join. Your visit may be exciting, and the members may be friendly and interesting, but no amount of warm personalities will make an omnivore comfortable in a vegan community or a lover of city amenities comfortable at a rural, off-grid ecovillage.

I am sure that members would have been eager to help had they only known what I needed.

Since this summer, I've dried off, grown up, and learned a lot about what it means to be a good visitor and a good host. Visiting communities (and hosting visitors at your own community) can yield some terrific experiences and fascinating new friends. If you pay attention to these and other tips and don't forget to bring a good attitude, you just may find the "utopia" you've been looking for!

Julie Pennington, co-editor of this issue, can be found on the front porch of House of Commons Co-op in Austin, Texas, preaching the power of community and eating Tofutti Cuties in bulk. julieepennington@hotmail.com.

SUSAN PATRICE

The Art and Ethics of Visitor Programs

By Blake Cothron

All around the world we're now witnessing an exciting upsurge of interest in intentional communities and alternative living arrangements. This is very promising news for any of us who are proponents of a more conscious, equitable, regenerative, and sane world. Major challenges face the intentional communities movement and any similar projects. The challenge I'd like to highlight now is the integration of new members and volunteers in a holistic, ethical, and meaningful way. We must ask, *what are we in our individual situations doing to provide an ethical, hospitable, meaningful, and fair introductory experience for newcomers in our community?*

How often have we in community witnessed the following scenario: an enthusiastic and good-natured new person is invited into your community who has useful skills, heart, and potential to contribute much to your community, but soon experiences internal challenges, becomes disheartened, and then departs? I've watched this drama unfold too many times (and been the disillusioned new person myself). As facilitators and creators of intentional communities we need to deeply consider why there is such a high turnover rate of potential new members and communitarians. We can start by first exploring a few crucial questions: why do people enthusiastically decide to explore membership in intentional community in the first place? Why do they often leave so soon? How can a visitor program better meet the holistic needs of new people and warmly integrate them into the community?

People choose to pursue intentional community life for many different reasons. Some are looking for a way out of the "rat race," and a simpler, more natural and holistic life. Others choose cooperative living to engage in educational or humanitarian work. Some wish to pursue their spiritual path while living with other seekers and practitioners of their faith. I think most can agree, however, that we basically all choose intentional community for very similar foundational reasons: we want deeper connections with other people and the Earth, more meaning in what we do, and to live a healthier, simpler, and more regenerative lifestyle. Personally, I chose to first explore community living in 2006 because I believed there had to be a much better way to live than I was experiencing in my struggling and crowded hometown. I craved a more integrated existence, simplicity, deeper relationships, involvement in organic agriculture, and living more in tune with nature.

I think it's important to remember how we all felt when we were first new to community. How did you feel? Were you excited, amazed, maybe a bit bewildered? Were you very open-hearted and generous, or were you quiet and reserved? I was a bit of all of those and also painfully idealistic and naïve. It's important for us to remember that joining a community is usually an enormous step out of the status quo and our privacy-addicted mindsets; it can be a culture shock. We can easily forget what it's like for a new person to join the group and how much of a dramatic internal shift they often must make to function cooperatively.

Sometimes we just *expect* them to understand what is to us common knowledge: why recycling is important, the virtues of not having a television, or the real dangers of GMO's, for example. We sometimes *expect* new people to *accept* our community lifestyles outright, with little to no time for adjustment. It's important to remember that anyone who is exploring intentional community is in the rare two percent or so of the population and deserves recognition and patience for that fact alone.

We must be real here and recognize that welcoming new people into our communities and farms is no simple task. It takes *much* time and effort to host someone properly, and even more consciousness and energy to create an integrated and holistic experience for them. And of course there are always some people who try, and then find out that community living is just not for them, or who are simply not good matches for the community. Yet the way we go about hosting someone will dramatically affect their experience and the likelihood of any future involvement in our community. What is often overlooked out of perceived practicality is the loving human touch and interaction, as well as practical arrangements like good housing and trying to match compatible people to your project, which makes all the difference.

Many times I traveled to a community as a prospective member or intern and experienced myself and others being treated like the means to a goal, and later on I also caught myself embarrassingly on the other end as well. It's all too easy to view new people, whether interns, apprentices, or prospective members, as energetic, free labor for all of our needy projects, and to treat them in that one-dimensional way. From experiences I had facilitating WWOOF volunteers in a farm community, I realized I had to become more sensitive to the fact that every person is a multi-dimensional being with different needs, desires, proclivities, fears, skills, dreams, and maturity level, and that interacting with them sensitively and respectfully is essential. We need to honor each person's journey and complex needs while treating them in a holistic way.

Too often I've seen rural communities operating like little boot camps with new people treated impersonally like "new recruits."

The first step, before we even *begin* to offer live-in programs in our communities, is to discern *why* we wish to begin a visitor program and how to best meet the needs of the visitors. Are we wanting to temporarily host someone simply to lend us a hand and teach them a skill, such as natural building, or are we offering an opportunity to explore potential membership? These two scenarios necessitate different strategies and arrangements. Depending on the purpose of the visit, we then can make arrangements to meet their basic needs and organize for their guidance from a community member or team.

Beyond this physical, basic level, I am advocating for the creation of a nurturing environment for interacting with a new person based on their multi-dimensional existence, so that they feel sustenance on many levels and both they and the community can better get their needs met. Let's explore some of the factors involved and how this holistic approach can be manifested.

In most successful community endeavors I will attest that effective communication is the foundation, and in general most deep, fulfilling relationships are based on open communication. So it's important to remember that people come to community generally seeking a more meaningful, fulfilling, and connected reality. The modern world is depressingly impersonal, as more computers, machines, and isolation prevent genuine human interaction and communication, even on a basic level. Integrating intimate, meaningful communication and sharing into a newcomer's stay is therefore vital. Imagine a new person being warmly welcomed over chai and relaxed casual conversation, instead of practical details and "breaking them in" with immediate work projects or orientations. How does the first option feel over the second?

We need to make sure we extend respect and warmth while fostering personal communication with new people. Too often I've seen rural communities operating like little boot camps with new people treated impersonally like "new recruits." The focus is on productivity, labor, and accomplishing goals, often for the benefit of a desired image or material aim. Personal development, reflection, spirituality, and emotional/artistic expression are curtailed in favor of pushing onward "the glorious mission." This is not a sustainable approach. We need to examine our community situations and *very honestly ask ourselves*, "are we collectively facilitating a sustainable, meaningful, and holistic experience for ourselves as well as newcomers?" Likewise we need to ask, "are our advertisements and outreach material accurate, up-to-date, or even *true*?"

Here's a story to dramatically illustrate this point: several years ago I found online a listing for a dynamic-sounding intentional community, complete with a dedicated group of conscious permaculture pioneers and an incredible organic mini-farm educational center overflowing with abundance and diversity. I was excited and scheduled my visit as an intern. As I pulled into the property backed dramatically by thousands of acres of steep, wild, dark, misty mountains; I was in awe of the beautiful setting. There indeed was an impressive diversity and abundance of fruit orchards and gardens...but what I quickly noticed an absence of was a *community*. The center was operated entirely by one man and his wife.

"Well," I figured, "this place is so amazing maybe it will still work out somehow." That evening I was shown my choices of housing. One was a dark, creaky, musty hundred-year old barn outfitted as a sort of dormitory, with lightbulbs hanging from the ceiling and raggedy old blankets and mattresses strewn about. The other option was a small, 8'x 8' unheated shack with gaps between the uninsulated wall boards just big enough to let the freezing March wind and snow blow inside during my first night. The "simple, organic diet" they offered consisted of nearly-spoilt dumpstered food, and the consensus decision making was made between the man and his wife. As *educational* as this center was, I left after about three days, feeling relieved to be gone yet disappointed and somewhat scattered.

It was not the cooperative and holistic community it was advertised as, and now I was very inconvenienced and hundreds of miles away from home and had to abruptly make new plans. The lesson for me was to not be naïve about trusting that a website is entirely accurate and honest, and to openly ask *a lot* of pertinent questions before making a move to a community. The online description of this community was 10 years old and obviously needed a lot of revision. Portraying our projects or community as something they are not is simply not ethical. Likewise, it's not ethical or useful to offer new people substandard housing and food or inhumane work and living arrangements, yet it's all too common.

The act of integrating new people into our communities is a delicate, sacred responsibility.

Now ask yourself, how would you feel being asked to eat and live in what is being offered to *your* interns or visitors? The fact that an arrangement is "livable" (sometimes survivable is more accurate) does not make it sustainable or humane. We need to extend our own human needs and desires to newcomers in community, who are vulnerable people as well. Let's be as generous as we can. Create living arrangements which are nice and inviting and foster a sense of privacy, safety, and nurturing. These things go a long way in helping a new person feel welcomed, appreciated, and respected, which will likely lead them to consider staying on longer.

As well as meeting basic physical needs, it's just as important to make an effort to meet the emotional and mental needs of a person. This is why I advocate scheduling a special time, perhaps once a week, to hold a "checking-in" session and ask them how their experience is going. How have they been feeling? What do they like best? What has been challenging? How has their image of the community changed so far? What is inspiring them? What would they change if they could? This could be done in a comfortable private room, over dinner, or in a nice natural setting. Try to facilitate it as a warm, personal exchange, not like a formal interview or going down a list of questions. And, unless necessary to do otherwise, keep their answers private or at least not completely public.

This small, simple exchange, I believe, can make a dramatic impact on a new person's feelings of connection and being cared for, as well as facilitate more internal clarity about their own experience. This will help not only them, but the community also, to have more clarity about how the visit is going and to help balance out any issues and potential problems early on.

Many times, new people will leave a community for very simple and often avoidable reasons. Lack of a private room, lack of vegan diet options, etc. can all be deal-breakers. Many times this can be avoided by clear communication and agreements beforehand. However, I'd say a majority of people leave community because of *lack of integration into the group*. Communities can become very close-knit or even form cliques that can be difficult or nearly impossible to penetrate, with new people often treated like outsiders. This can be avoided by inviting new folks to community events, meals, and outings. Allow them to introduce themselves in front of everyone and share a bit about themselves. Host an open mic or talent show and encourage them to express their artistic sides. Have fun! If they express interest, facilitate a small personal project for them; perhaps painting the kitchen or planting a fruit tree. This will help them feel a sense of contribution and meaning—innate human needs.

The act of integrating new people into our communities is a delicate, sacred responsibility. We want new people to feel positive about joining our communities. Both parties are taking a risk. They are trusting us to facilitate a good experience for them; to keep them safe and nurtured, and to offer them what we have advertised. We want them in turn to have a positive, dynamic, and educational experience, and contribute to and potentially join our community. We all want to get our needs met by the whole event.

I admit, I'm still an idealist. I do not mean to offend those who offer well-meaning, but still deficient visitor programs. I believe that integrating even one (or more) of these suggestions into your visitor program will dramatically improve the experience of your visitors and lead to better outcomes for everyone involved. In summary, I'd like to highlight these important points:

Be Honest: Make sure any outreach material is accurate, honest, and up-to-date. Be *very clear, honest, and descriptive* about the housing situation, food quality, daily schedule, spirituality or religious focus, privacy, fees, local climate, mission of the community, alcohol/tobacco use, and the communities' basic expectations of visitors. Ambiguity leads to problems, disappointments, and chaos.

Be Fair: Make sure your situation is nurturing and balanced for a *multi-dimensional person*. Share decent housing that is clean, heatable, at least somewhat private, and that feels cozy and safe. If all you have available is sub-par, make that very clear, and post pictures of it. Create their schedule to be livable and not arduous. Allow at least *one full day* per week of off-time for rest and reflection, ideally with no expectations of their attending anything. If you are to charge something, take into account all the labor they will be doing.

Connect: Welcome new people warmly and stay in close communication with them throughout their stay. Get to know them and engage the new person in events and outings. Have a friendly, personal, and private meeting time with them at least once during their stay to check in and connect. Be sensitive to their needs, varying moods, and desires. People usually join community because they want more connection, meaning, and deeper relationships.

Create space for new people to express themselves and contribute: If they show an interest in a personal project or contribution, try to help them to do it. Keep it small and realistic. Share opportunities for art, music, dance, and recreation.

Be Real: Be open about (at least some of) the challenges and issues facing the community. Be open and real about the mission, focus, and mood of the community, and expect openness from them as well. Learn from each other and be accepting of their enthusiasm and a fresh, new perspective on your community. ❧

***Editor's Note:** We invite responses from communitarians to the questions and concerns Blake presents in this article. We'd like to present a diversity of perspectives on the issues raised, and you can help with that. Please let us know what you think.*

Blake Cothron is an artist, writer, organic agriculturist, and holistic life teacher, currently founding the Vedic Living Farm project in Kentucky. He practices Ayurvedic medicine, Goddess worship, and Ashtanga Yoga, and can be reached at healandserve@gmail.com.

BY JULIE PENNINGTON

Planning a Community Visit

ROD RYLANDER

ROD RYLANDER

People visit intentional communities because they're curious about community living, or to get ideas about land, work systems, or meeting facilitation for example, or to take workshops on community-related topics such as conflict resolution, permaculture, or meditation. However, the majority of people visiting communities do so because they're seeking one to join themselves. If you consider all that you could learn from visiting a community, it's possible to fulfill more than one purpose during your stay.

You may already have a sense of community living and may already know of several communities you'd like to investigate. Ask yourself what intrigues you about communities and what in particular you like about the communities you've heard of. What questions do you have about community living in general? Write your questions and concerns down and use them as a starting point to find out more.

The *Communities Directory* is probably the most useful resource for the initial criteria-gathering stage of the process. Flip through the *Directory's* cross-reference chart and become familiar with some of the points you'll want to consider in your search: location, purpose, population, decision-making style, shared or independent income, diet, substance use, and so on. Also check out the "Communities Seeking Members" ads in the back of *Communities* magazine.

Make a list of personal priorities. Are you looking for an ecovillage, a back-to-the-land-style rural group, an income-sharing commune, a cohousing neighborhood, or an urban co-op? Are spirituality, diet and health lifestyle, relationship style, or gender orientation most important to you? What kind of financial investment could you make to a group? As you ask these and other questions, consider your current lifestyle. What are the aspects of your life that give you happiness and fulfillment? What are the aspects you would most like to change? Be realistic and try to recognize those things that you don't want to live without or those things you most want to give up. In my own case, for example,

The more you know about what you're looking for, the easier it will be to plan your trip.

what I love about my life at my co-op in Austin is the opportunity to abstain from eating animal products, enjoy local live music several nights a week, and the warm climate. This helped me set parameters for my search, such as geographic regions with a warm climate, proximity to a major city's cultural life, and places with a vegan-friendly diet. I'm uncomfortable with my dependence on cars, so I might keep my eyes open for a community with a car co-op or one small enough to bike around.

The more you know about what you're looking for, the easier it will be to plan your trip. This is also a great place to start a communities journal, like Sue Stone did. *(See "Excerpt from a Community Seeker's Journal," pg. 29.)* Write down all of your priorities now. It will be useful to reflect on them later (and after visiting many communities, some of them might change).

Now that you have an idea of your search criteria, it's time to start finding some communities that might suit you well. You'll find links to individual community listings on the websites of the Fellowship for Intentional Community (FIC), publishers of this magazine *(ic.org)*; Ecovillage Network of the Americas *(ena@gaia.org)*; and the Cohousing Association of the U.S. *(cohousing.org)*.

If you cannot find a website for a particular kind of community, don't assume that such a community doesn't exist or isn't worth visiting (maybe they just don't have a website). Again, use the cross-reference chart, the map, and the index in the *Communities Directory* to hone your options. If you have time, attend a communities conference such as an FIC regional gathering, Twin Oaks' annual communities gathering over Labor Day weekend, The Farm's new conference in May, or a Northwest Intentional Communities Association gathering, to meet community representatives and find out more. Mention to acquaintances in the communities movement that you are planning a visit and see what they have to offer. Ask if your friends know anyone at the communities that interest you. Gather information and make a list of pros and cons of each of those top several communities that seem to most closely match your needs. Then ask members of these communities if the facts you have are still accurate. Keep in mind that communities are made up of individuals. When the membership changes in small communities, it is likely that at least some aspects of the group also change. Make sure that the groups you are considering visiting are open to hosting guests.

Begin contacting communities several months before you'd like to visit. Many groups have set times that they are open or closed to visitors, so keep your travel dates flexible. Don't assume that they will be able to fit your schedule (although if they are, remember to acknowledge their accommodation). Also consider how much time you can afford to take off work for your trip and how much time you will need to accomplish your goals at each community. While planning my own long communities tour, I felt that I needed at least five days at each place, and this estimate worked well for me. I was searching for a community to join, but if you have different reasons for visiting communities, you might want more or less time than this.

It is a good idea to visit at least two communities on any given trip. It will help your perspective and make the most efficient use of your travel time. If you find one or two communities that you definitely want to visit, open up the *Communities Directory* to the maps section and draw a line between the two places and see which other communities may be roughly near the route. Even if you had no interest in some of these groups during your original research, consider them again. Every group of people living intentionally together has something to teach the community seeker. You might want to use communities along your route as rest stops in which to reflect on the previous community visit and prepare for the next. A spiritual retreat community with hot springs among cozy cabins would make for a great rest stop!

When contacting communities to request a visit, follow the community's suggestions described in their *Directory* listing or on their website. In your letter or email message introduce yourself and tell the group how you heard about them and why you are interested in visiting; for example, that you're considering potential membership or in just learning more about community. Ask about their visitor policy. If you know someone at the community or even a friend-of-a-friend, mention this connection. Tell briefly about your experience, skills, or interests, and any special needs you may have. Provide contact information for someone to get back to you, and, if it's a snail-mailed letter, include a self-addressed stamped envelope. By enclosing a photo of yourself, a sketch, or something else that will make your letter unique and memorable, you are more likely to ensure a prompt response. Remember that some communities may get many requests to host visitors, or answer their correspondence infrequently, so don't be frustrated if you don't get an answer right away—one reason you should allow ample time to plan before your visit. If you don't receive a response from the group in two to three

Ask if it is a convenient time to ask about the community.

weeks, try another approach. If you've emailed, you might just send another email. If you've sent a letter, a phone call might be a better way to catch someone. Be considerate of the group and if you must call, try to do so in early evening rather than late at bedtime or first thing in the morning when members may be busy getting ready for work.

When you make contact with your potential hosts, they may or may not tell you everything you need to know about your visit. Many groups will send a letter describing what to expect on your visit and what you should plan to bring with you. If the group is not forthcoming with these tips, make sure and ask plenty of questions. What special items should you pack? What might the weather be like at that time of year? Will you need bug spray, a rain poncho, a flashlight? Be sure to find out where you will be staying and if you should bring a tent or sleeping bag. Are children and pets welcome with visitors? Will your diet be accommodated? What is the best way to get to the community? Can you provide your own transportation? What are the parking rules? What is an appropriate amount of money to cover your expenses? Who should you direct further questions to? Will this person be your host when you arrive?

While hosting visitors is often enjoyable for the community, it can also be a lot of work. The group would not open its home to strangers if it had nothing to gain. What can you do, then, to make your stay a mutually beneficial experience? Find out why this group is open to visitors in the first place. They may be looking for new members, but they might also need help with work, want to spread their philosophy, gain income from guest fees, or simply enjoy the motivation of having new people to spend time with. *(See "Guess Who's Coming to Dinner?," pg. 43.)*

Many communities need help with work. You might offer to do those mundane tasks that make community members groan (think washing dishes). Also bring old clothes and your work gloves, in case they need help hauling brush, stacking firewood, or other outdoor jobs. It's a nice gesture to bring a gift if you can, but be sensitive to the culture of the community when choosing what to bring (don't present home-brew to a substance-free community, for example). Try to bring either something functional from their wish list or a nice treat everyone can enjoy. Offer any special skills or talents you have. If you are a musician, offer to play a concert; if you're an artist, offer to create a piece for them or decorate a wall. Be creative.

Don't pretend that the community is exactly what you are looking for if it isn't.

Let's assume that you and your host have been in contact several times, you've made specific arrangements, and you're ready to be on your way. The time you spend traveling there, by bus, shared vehicle, or plane, is perfect for pulling out your community-visiting journal. Write what you know and like or dislike about what you've heard of the community, any questions you want to remember to ask its members, and your expectations.

When you arrive at the community, you will likely get a tour and be shown a room, dorm space, or campground in which to set up your temporary home away from home. You should know who your main liaison in the community is, as that person can fill you in on mealtimes, community happenings, and any labor assignments they may have planned for you. If you don't have labor assignments, take the initiative to jump in and help wherever you see a need. The group may not have work and activities planned for your entire stay, so use this time to relax, get a feel for the community, talk to members, and reflect on your surroundings. It is a good idea to set aside time for journaling while you are there. Write about what you do, see, and feel. There is a lot to remember about the community you visit, so record facts for review later. Because food and diet are especially important to me, writing down what each community served at dinner helped me to recall memories and how I felt during each stay.

Talk to a variety of members, and remember the golden rule of "asking to ask." Before dumping a mass of questions on someone, ask if it is a convenient time to ask about the community. Don't be offended if the honest answer is "No." What for you is a vacation spot is really someone's home, and members have responsibilities and lives of their own that they will have to address. If you meet someone you are particularly interested in speaking with but they're too busy to talk, you might ask when a better time might be. Helping a community member to garden, wash dishes, or perform other tasks can also be a great time to chat about the community, if the member is comfortable doing so.

In addition to the questions you have already thought of, you can ask how a particular member came to be a part of the community, what she likes and dislikes about it, and how she feels they have addressed their vision as a group. Asking different members what they feel the community's priorities are will give you a good perspective on the group's diversity and their overall adherence to goals. You can also ask what different members find challenging in the community, or what they'd most like to improve or change.

After you return home, consider sending a thank you note. It makes community members feel good, helps reward them for the sometimes arduous task of hosting visitors, and may help them remember you kindly if you decide to return to learn more.

The most important thing to remember during your stay, however, is to be honest with yourself and with the group. It is easy to become enchanted with many aspects of community life, but you should remember what you are looking for and objectively evaluate how the particular group and setting mesh with your personal vision. Definitely put your best foot forward and be gracious, but don't pretend that the community is exactly what you are looking for if it isn't. Neither seekers nor communities benefit from gaining new members who aren't a good fit. If you don't find your dream home during the visit, you probably wouldn't be happy there as a member. Hopefully, though, the community you visit may turn out to be exactly what you have been looking for. Either way, plan it out and make the most of your opportunity to be part of the magic of community. Good luck!

Julie Pennington, co-editor of this issue, and veteran community visitor, lives at a co-op community in Austin, Texas.

Author Julie Pennington.

e Stone and Geoff Stone.

Excerpts from a Community Seeker's Journal

BY SUE STONE

From 1994 through 1998, Sue and Geoff Stone, who had lived in Ozark, Arkansas for 14 years, visited dozens of communities looking for one to join. Here are excerpts from Sue's journal, with her personal observations and insights of the sometimes inspiring, sometimes arduous, community-seeking process.

December, 1994, Missouri.

On Winter Solstice weekend in December Geoff and I visited a small community on 75 acres in Missouri I'll call Warm Springs. We felt comfortable there soon after we arrived. The couple who'd invited us, Sam and Debra (not their real names) seemed genuinely interested in us and our ideas and experiences. It was easy to talk with them and we seemed to have a lot in common.

When we first arrived, I was surprised to see just an ordinary little house. We had tea with Sam and their two boys, who were making pumpkin pies in a toaster oven. The boys took us on a tour. It was pretty land, but there wasn't much there in terms of physical infrastructure: a shed for outdoor cooking, a teepee, a sweat lodge, a children's fort. The home-schooled boys were impressive: mature, knowledgeable, serious.

Saturday I helped Debra fix up the teepee and Geoff helped Sam prepare the sweat lodge. Debra took me on a short hike to a spring. She told me about the women's group that meets there, and showed me the women's altar. She told me about how they had lived in a teepee when the boys were small.

Saturday night was what community is about for me. Other people arrived, includin another couple, Roger and Sarah, an their son, and two men from St. Loui We had a potluck dinner, talked, an played drums. Geoff and I talked a lo with Roger, who actually owns the lan He had lived at Ananda Village in Cal

The bathroom was a choice between an indoor toilet which didn't flush or a long walk to a cold outhouse.

fornia, and told us about that communit He was excited to learn about Geoff greenhouse, and I got the feeling that w would really be an asset to their community, if we chose to go there.

The solstice ceremony was held aroun a fire. We lit candles and spoke of our feelings about the past fall and the coming o the winter and the new year. We went int the teepee and talked and played drums That night Geoff and I slept in our tent at least tried to, as it was really too cold t sleep well. The moon was full, and w were beside the creek and I could hear i all night.

The weekend was hard in a lot of ways The bathroom situation was a problem, choice between an indoor toilet which didn't flush or a long walk to a cold outhouse. I was tired from not getting enough sleep, and felt grubby and uncomfortable and cold much of the time. And there was also the unknown: What i going to happen next, and when, an what will it be like?

A new guest came the next day for th sweat lodge ceremony to be held tha afternoon. I liked hanging aroun inside near the stove that morning talking and drinking coffee. One visitor was a musician, a drummer another was a young man fron Syria. The third was a storyteller very interesting and personable They were all so nice—friendly warm, interested in us and seemingly glad to have us there.

KIMCHI RYLANDER

I kept crying at the ceremonies. It all felt so right to me. I felt awkward and uncomfortable and apprehensive, and yet like it was where I wanted and needed to be. Even though Geoff and I couldn't stay for the entire sweat lodge ceremony, I loved it and I felt wonderful afterwards, and I felt so loved and appreciated. They thanked us for being there!

What I really appreciated about these people was their dedication and commitment to the land. Sam wants to respect the land as the Native Americans do, and do the celebrations and ceremonies to honor it and work with it. Sarah worked with Starhawk and does rituals with women's groups. The group also wants to have a garden and passive solar houses. And they have already worked hard to build good relationships with the local community.

They'd like to buy more land adjacent to their property. I could see us being part of that, and helping to buy that land. The problems I could see with this community are that there doesn't seem to be much opportunity for getting jobs outside, and the land is pretty isolated. Also, it would be a small community. They are only two hours from St. Louis, so that is a resource for people and a market for products or services. What I liked best about it was the people, the Earth ceremonies, and their dedication to the land. It seemed like a definite possibility.

I kept crying at the ceremonies. It all felt so right to me.

January, 1995, Arkansas.

A few weeks later we visited Thomas (not his real name), who plans to start a community on his small parcel of land in the crystal-mining area of Arkansas outside of Hot Springs. We were there to take his workshop on ferro-cement construction and attend his birthday party.

His land is really pretty, and has a nice, year-round stream. I found Thomas a kind, interesting, and talented guy. I enjoyed walking in the hills, learning to do ferro-cement work, and talking with him and his friends. The party was another taste of how I imagine community would be: good music, really interesting conversation, and especially drumming by candlelight. I felt so good after that weekend, energized yet relaxed.

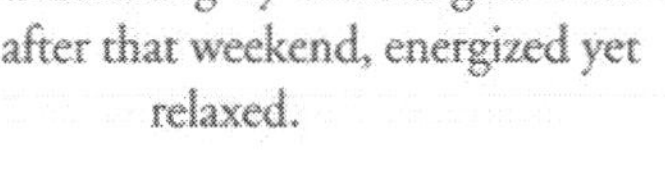

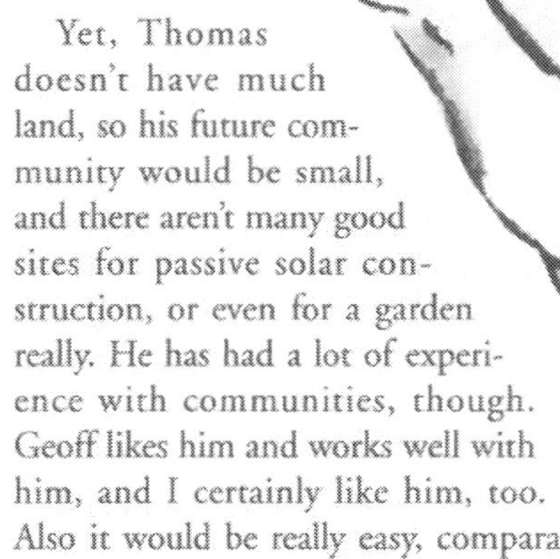

Yet, Thomas doesn't have much land, so his future community would be small, and there aren't many good sites for passive solar construction, or even for a garden really. He has had a lot of experience with communities, though. Geoff likes him and works well with him, and I certainly like him, too. Also it would be really easy, comparatively, to get started there, certainly much easier than moving somewhere farther away. But "easy" is not what the community search is about. It's about what we want, whatever that is!

February, 1995, Massachusetts.

First day. We're here at Sirius Community in Massachusetts, and it's beautiful! The main community building is made with all this hand-hewn natural wood. The guest area is like a sort of rustic cabin, but really comfortable. Separate rooms lead off a hallway sitting area, with a wood stove and a place to fix tea. Best of all: three showers, several toilets and a bathtub! We've had a shower and a rest and I feel normal again, more or less.

We have pretty much concluded that a nearby community we just visited, Gaia (not their real name), is too activist-oriented for us. They love their land but otherwise seem so focused on saving the world that organizing and maintaining their own community seem to be neglected. And I really didn't sense the central focus.

I expect Sirius to be different. It is much more physically comfortable, of course, but it is 16 years old, so they've had more time to get it together. Anyway, it is nice to be here, finally. I expect I'll want to join and already I'm trying to figure out how it could be done. I guess I should just "be here now" for the present.

Second day, morning. Dinner last night felt like my concept of what community is all about: people sitting around a table after a meal, talking and sharing, then working together to clean up afterwards. Dinner began with everyone standing silently in a circle holding hands. Everything here starts that way. We saw a slide show about Sirius and introduced ourselves, met some members, and had an orientation.

I slept really well and feel pretty good today. I still think I'd prefer my own bathroom, but I guess I might eventually get used to this down-the-hall set-up. Other members besides the guests use the bathrooms here, and there is no gender designation, so you might be washing up or showering or using the toilet next to someone of the opposite sex. Of course, the toilets and showers have doors, and usually there isn't anyone else there, but it still seems strange.

In some ways Sirius doesn't fit my concept of a community, as most of its members don't live here. It seems more like a church. You pay dues to belong and donate eight hours of work a week. You might rent living space here, or get it somewhere nearby. You have to earn your own living somehow. There are shared meals, but you have to subscribe to them, and take your turn supplying and cooking a meal. You can pay $25 a month for a share of garden produce, and $20 to use community bulk foods. It's not like the sort of community where everyone lives together. But they are, nevertheless, working toward goals which are similar to ours.

"Easy" is not what the community search is about. It's about what we want, whatever that is!

Second day, afternoon. So far I feel really good here. Right now I'd love to stay forever. After breakfast we had a tour. Breakfast (and meals in general) are in the farmhouse, the original building here. There's a kitchen and a living/dining room with a wood stove, a few chairs and couches, and three long tables, with windows looking out over the garden. It's cozy and neat, though well-used. Also, there is a library and a bulletin board. People hang out there before and after meals. Before meals and before going off to work projects everyone stands and holds hands in silence for a few minutes, to "realize oneness." There's a short blessing before meals, sometimes announcements, and the menu. After meals, they discuss what work needs to be done.

After the tour we spent two hours in a meeting where we were told how Sirius operates. I got the feeling that the only way to get here would be to move to the area and find some way to live, and meanwhile spend months or years working through the membership process. I was told later that "exploring members" can rent space here, assuming it's available and that you have enough income. Anyway, it's not as hard as I thought it would be. The people are so nice—warm, friendly, helpful. I'm sure there are problems at times, but they all seem happy and relaxed. I haven't noticed anyone rushing around or looking stressed.

Again at lunch it was relaxed and congenial, lots of interesting conversation. People just pitch in and help clean up, and it seems to go quickly and smoothly. After lunch, I helped with a mailing at the farmhouse, and Geoff helped with firewood. I went for a walk on the trail through the woods.

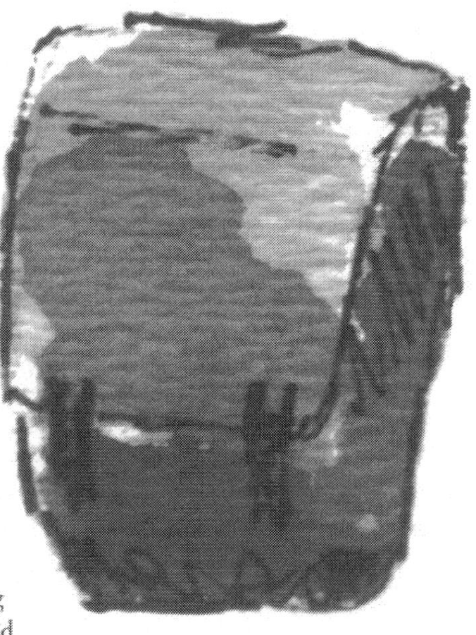

Every place I've been so far I can [imag]gine myself living, so I guess I can't be [sur]e my feelings at this point are a reliable [gau]ge. After one day, how can I really have [eno]ugh informa[tion]? This is really [my] first opera[tion]al community [I've] experienced. I [can't] keep thinking [ho]w good it [wou]ld be to live here. But there are disad[van]tages; for example, housing costs seem [dou]ble those in Arkansas, and there aren't [ma]ny jobs close by. It would be a half-[hou]r commute to get to work, most likely. [An]d part of the reason for community [livi]ng is to get away from that stuff! [Th]ere's a possibility of a job here in the [com]munity, perhaps, or a business oper[atin]g out of the community eventually. [So] it might work out, if we really wanted [to b]e here.

Dinner last night felt like my concept of what community is all about.

Third day, evening. Geoff and I spent [some] time before dinner discussing pros and [con]s and possibilities. We just go around [and] around and back and forth. I am [alr]eady tired of the uncertainty, but I [gue]ss it will go on anyway!

Last night one of the founding mem[ber]s, Bruce, gave a talk on the role of [com]munity in the modern world. He said [the]re is typically a breakdown of the forms [and] structures in society, then a period of [cha]os. Then comes a time of creation of a [mu]ltitude of possibilities for new forms [and] structures, after which there is sud[den]ly a "quantum leap" to a new form, a [ne]w level. He talked about how it is easier [to] grow and evolve and expand one's con[sci]ousness in a supportive and energized [en]vironment such as Sirius. He talked [ab]out how living outside is oppressive and [can] tend to hold one down and prevent [one']s expansion, unless the person is very [str]ong and evolved. This struck such a [cho]rd with me—that is exactly how living [in] Ozark feels to me!

After breakfast I had a massage with a [wo]man who lives here, and it felt so good! [Th]en I joined in for part of the circle [da]ncing, in the new octagonal meeting [ha]ll. I kept looking around the room, at [th]e people, the beautiful building, the woods outside, thinking, "I'm really here! I'm dancing at Sirius!"

There was a meditation before lunch. There was one yesterday, too, a half-hour "meditation for planetary healing." At lunch there were several visitors, as today was Open House, and the dining area was really crowded. Everyone managed to get fed and find a seat and there were several shifts for the dish-washing and cleanup. After lunch we had a closing meeting, where everyone, including the leaders from the guest department, shared their thoughts and feelings about the weekend. I said I was impressed by the care everyone seems to take with everything—people, buildings, dishes, etc.—and that it feels very good being here.

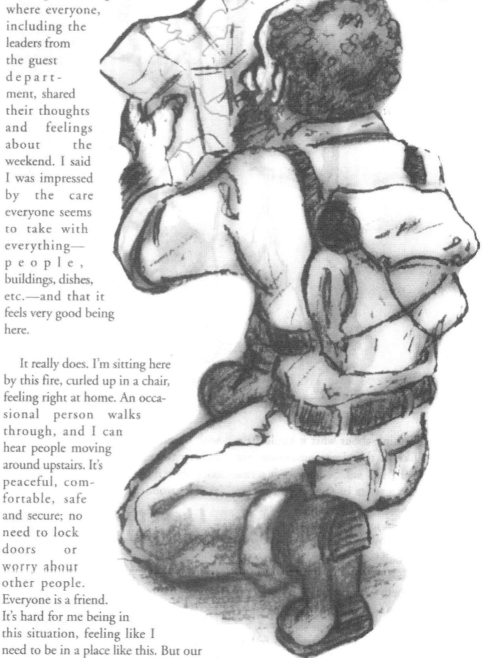

It really does. I'm sitting here by this fire, curled up in a chair, feeling right at home. An occasional person walks through, and I can hear people moving around upstairs. It's peaceful, comfortable, safe and secure; no need to lock doors or worry about other people. Everyone is a friend. It's hard for me being in this situation, feeling like I need to be in a place like this. But our search is about what Geoff and I both want, not just about what I want. If it were just me I'd try to find a way to be here at Sirius, but it's not just me. It could be another four years before Geoff is ready to do this. I hope it doesn't take that long! I wish we could just stay here.

I know I can't know enough in two days to be sure this would be the right place. I may visit others that are as good, or better. But I've spent 14 years of my life in Ozark and I'm tired of it! While there have been good times and I've grown and learned a lot, some-

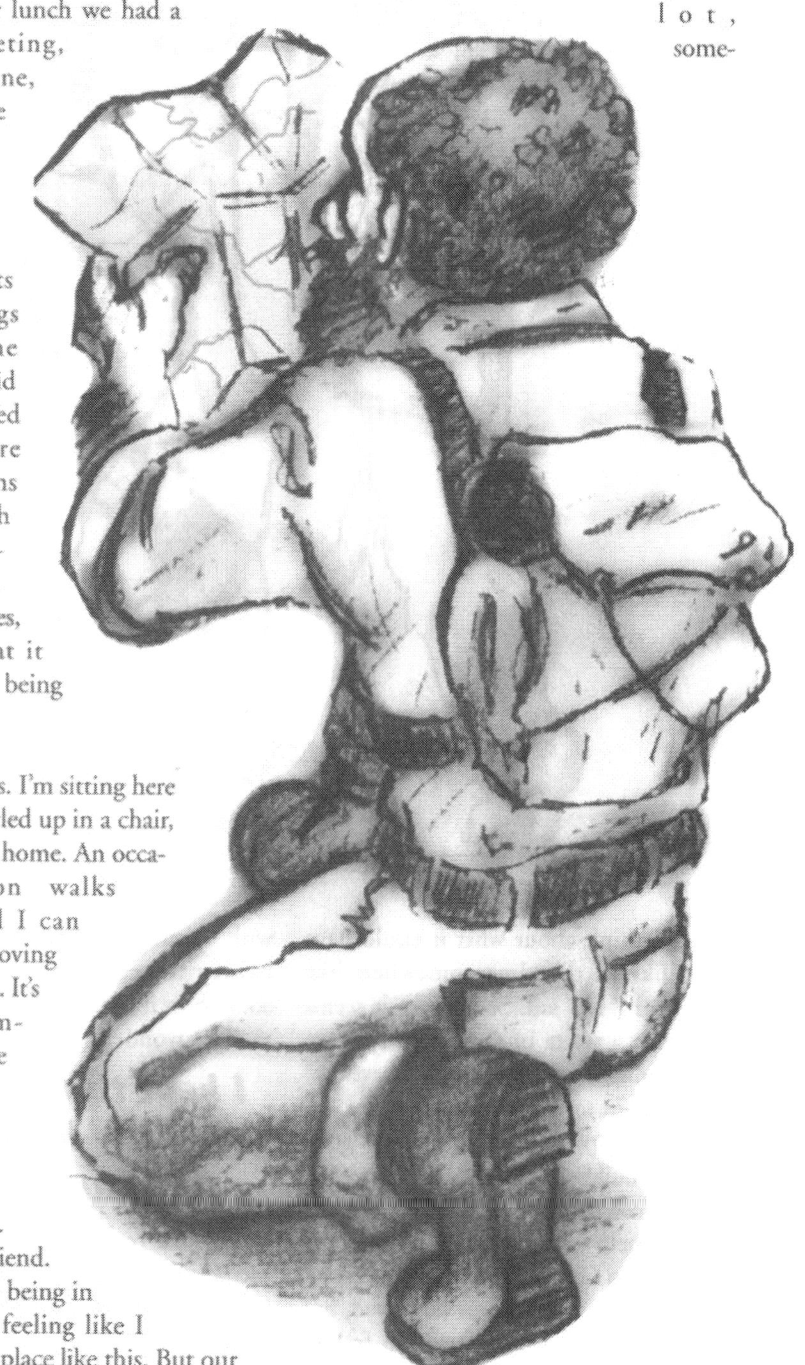

times I think about what it could have been like all this time, somewhere like this, and I feel sad. Sometimes it seems like such a waste of time to not live in community, and how much do I have left? I don't want to waste any more time.

Fourth day, morning. Geoff has gone with the building crew to do some logging. He'll be coming back early to help fix lunch and I'll help with that. I decided to stay here and go for a walk, then take it easy.

Last night's dinner was very good, but there wasn't much conversation for us. The members sat together, and we were with the interns. It was comfortable and homey there, though. I was thinking about how it would be if we joined a community, wondering how long it would be

I kept thinking, "I'm really here! I'm dancing at Sirius!"

before we really had friends and felt included. It seems easy for me to feel left out and not part of things. I know people enjoy being with friends and carrying on their relationships, and it's not the same when new people are there, so I understood the situation. But I expect it might be hard at first in a community, like moving anywhere.

It's probably been good being here the extra days. On the weekend the guest department people were here for us, and there were four of them and six of us, so they'd be around at meals, etc., to talk to us and answer questions. Now people are going about their normal business, and there aren't many of them. Most work outside, and only a few work here, so it's pretty deserted and quiet. If the building w were working today on the confer- e center there would be lots of noise t door, but they are out logging. We e to find our own ways of being, ich is more real.

I love this place, and I long to part of something like this. ing here, though, would prob- y involve working outside the mmunity, at least for several rs. I have been feeling that prefer a place where more ople actually lived and worked the community. That may ppen here eventually. There is talk of ilding more member housing, com- nity businesses, a larger greenhouse, d expanded guest housing. Right now, ough, it would be more like moving to new town in the ordinary way. You'd ve to find a job, locate housing, and so th. But you'd live here, or near here, d participate in the activities, work and eals and food sharing. It would be a od life, a large improvement on Ozark. t I'm not sure it is what we were pic- ring when we came up with this idea to e in community. We'll see, I guess, en we visit East Wind, what it's like to e in a community where people live and rk all the time.

They talk here sometimes about how u can "create community" anywhere u live, and that community is not nec- sarily living with other people. Someone o said it's not so important what is complished in a physical sense in com- unity but how it's done—the ationships and growth and learning of ople. It's respect for your tools and your rroundings. It's your own growth and arning, peace of mind and spiritual cus that is important. It's the journey at matters, not the destination.

Fourth day, afternoon. I ended up aking most of lunch, mixed together a few batches of leftover beans, made some cornbread, and found some apples. Geoff made some salad with

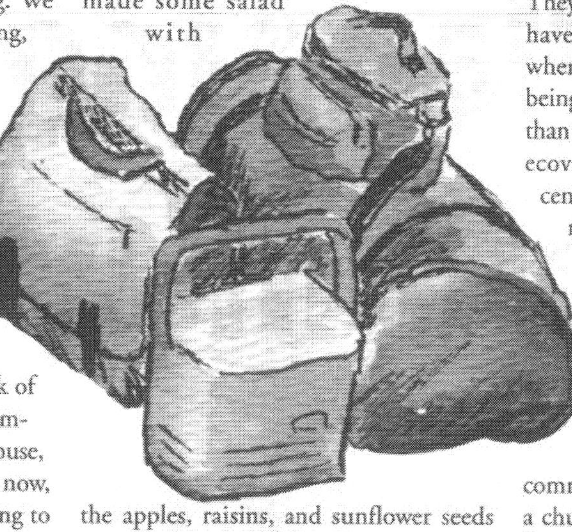

the apples, raisins, and sunflower seeds when he got back. Another member was there, fortunately, to find a recipe and give suggestions. It gave me another taste of what community life would be like. Geoff went back to help with the logging again. I guess he is doing my four hours of work for today. Most of what is going on today

Sometimes it seems like such a waste of time to not live in community, and how much do I have left?

is with the apprentices and a couple of members only. It seems like most of the work on the building and in the garden gets done by apprentices, as the members usually work only eight hours a week. I have decided to spend my last afternoon taking it easy, reading and writing. Hauling brush might be more fun, but this is my last day of vacation—might as well re-create!

New members, a family from the West Coast, live near us in this building, The father does carpentry, so he can earn a living anywhere. They have two young children and have been here five months. They probably aren't going to stay. They have decided they want a community where people mainly live together, that being the main focus and purpose, rather than as it is at Sirius, with the focus on the ecovillage, gardening, and conference center. This place doesn't suit them. Too much energy goes into the various projects, they said, rather than into real community living. In a way, I agree. It all seems quite scattered here. It's a nice place, but where is the community? I do understand the idea that "community" takes different forms, and this is a community in many ways, somewhat like a church is, but more so, because of the gardening and meal-sharing. But I think Geoff and I are looking for more than this in terms of people living together. Though we also want the gardening and sustainable living parts, too. Maybe we just won't find exactly what we want. Maybe we will have to create it ourselves ultimately, somehow. I'm sorry what I'm seeking isn't here. But I guess it's still a possibility. It'll be awhile before we are ready, and Sirius is still evolving.

Sue and Geoff Stone eventually found their community home in Earthaven Ecovillage in North Carolina, which they joined in 1999. Sue has been active on the membership and airspinning (minutes and decisions) committees, and Geoff on the finance committee.

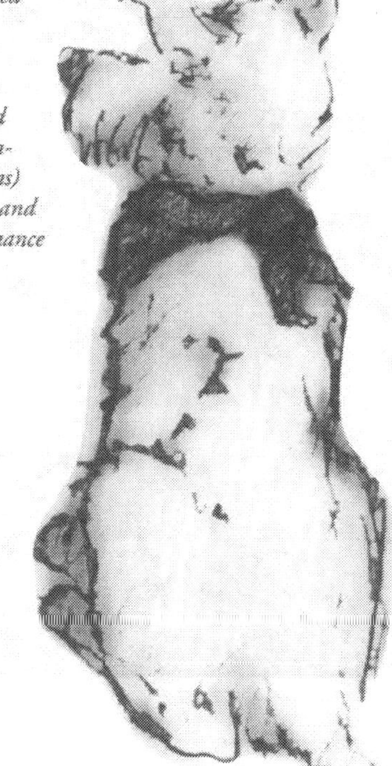

The author on day three of a desert solo vision quest, part of his apprenticeship program at Lost Valley Educational Center in Oregon.

THE Dilettante's JOURNEY

~ PART I ~

How do you pick a community to join if you're interested in . . . EVERYTHING?

BY FRANK BEATY

"yanked up my 5,000th root of the day. This one loosened and slid out of the dirt without a fight. I stood up and stretched my back. The sun was hotter than hell, and I ew there'd be a headache later, no matter how much water lrank. I was out of shape for this kind of work.

I saw Farmer, one of my hosts at Earthaven, balancing on beam of his barn's new roof. I could tell from two hundred rds that he was smiling at me, checking in. I lifted both ms and released a "Wahoo!" I was blistered, burning up, d out in the field alone, but I was having a blast. I could hear me lively music coming from the boom box and tried to ess who it might be. Phish, maybe? I wondered briefly if ey always listened to jam bands around here.

So this was Earthaven. I'd heard of this ecovillage for years id followed some of its progress with interest. Finally I was ere, and better yet, I'd discovered the Gateway project.

Gateway Field was new at Earthaven. fter the morning tour, Clark, the ur guide, had told me he suspected would enjoy working with this par- cular gang. Earthaven had always emed to have everything going for —courses, businesses, at least two rious quarterly publications, and ie whole place was off-grid—but it ever had a farm. And for me, no ommunity without one would ever do. Now I was clearing ots from several acres of freshly cleared topsoil, a forest just vo weeks earlier, which lay between a sparkling stream on one de and a brand new barn-in-progress on the other.

I have told myself and others, like a mantra, that I aim to someday live in intentional community.

I came in for a break and Farmer, 31, gave me a quick tour f his and his 21-year-old partner Brian's state-of-the-art tool iop, complete with every construction tool they would ever eed. Oh, and did I mention the shop was solar-powered? h, and did I tell you it was inside a former U-Haul truck? h, and did I say the truck runs on biodiesel? I marveled at their iper-rig and wondered how the hell these young home- uilders afforded it.

Farmer pointed to the perfect spans of timber they were sing for the barn's frame and said he'd negotiated them for ee from a local lumber operation, which would otherwise urn, dump, or chip these "mill ends" as waste. He explained that he and Brian had raised the money to buy and equip the truck from building homes for other Earthaven members, and raised most of the Gateway project money from multiple friendly loans from community members, with no collateral. "For ten years I've wanted to clear some acres and start a farm," he said, smiling. "This is my dream."

He mentioned that the band I'd heard earlier was not Phish, but Widespread Panic. Then he added, "But we don't just listen to jam bands around here." We got back to work—Brian and Farmer bickering on the roof, another visitor-helper and I standing below, hoisting up metal roofing and laughing at them.

I have told myself and others, like a mantra, that I aim to someday live in intentional community. I have read books and articles, watched documentaries, and traveled around the country to learn more about them. My values continue to evolve away from those of unsustainable cities and toward those of most intentional communities. I have enrolled in courses and even taken jobs that I hoped might lead me into the bosom of intentional community. But here I am, eight years later, still hanging out in Los Angeles.

My mother looked at me once and said matter-of-factly, "You're a dilettante." I was stung, and went straight to the dictionary to confirm that she was indeed calling me an indolent, decadent, grape-eating faux-aristocrat. She explained that she had simply observed me as something of a dabbler, a sampler of life. While the dictionary does offer some of the more scathing definitions I feared, I have come to understand what she meant. As you'll see, the way I conducted my search for community only proves her point.

Lost Valley

The Dilettante got his feet wet at Lost Valley Educational Center in Dexter, Oregon, in the summer of 1998. I'd learned about the apprenticeship program by way of an encounter with their lovely quarterly, Talking Leaves. I knew nothing of intentional communities and couldn't even imagine the physical environs of such a place, but Lost Valley's Apprenticeship

Program seemed the perfect antidote to my Los Angeles malaise. There I could slake my thirst for meaning, which had come to a ridiculous, raging boil.

I fired off an impassioned application for the program, confessing that for years as an actor I had been little more than a pretty-faced pitch-man for pharmaceuticals, detergents, booze, and even the British beef industry (I was the last beef spokesman before the outbreak of mad cow disease in England). I needed redemption. I wanted to change my life. Please accept me into your heavenly hippie home, et cetera. By early June, I was shopping for supplies and packing my bags.

Brian Love of the Gateway Field project, whom the author worked with during his stay at Earthaven Ecovillage in North Carolina.

Somewhere around Fresno, my vehicle vomited oil all over the interstate and broke down at a gas station. I broke down myself, blubbering and wondering just what the hell I had done with my life. Somehow I managed to sleep, right there in that buzzing parking lot, my first night ever in my brand new (30-year-old) VW camper. Leaving my shitty life in L.A. was going to be even lonelier and more terrifying than I'd imagined.

Somehow I made it to Lost Valley, and the land's loveliness unraveled itself: sunny fields, gardens, meadows, streams, fir and cedar forests, cabin clusters, yurts, teepees, a solar shower, sheep, chickens, and children. The residents greeted me quietly, sweetly, but I could tell they were excited about the arrival of this new batch of summer apprentices. Julie, a tall, gentle, lovely woman maybe a little older than me, looked into my eyes and furrowed her brow.

"You're very different from how I imagined." I guess she'd formed some ideas from the L.A. actor's essay.

"Maybe it's the shaved head," I replied, smiling. Right now I looked more like Shel Silverstein than George Clooney. I wasn't exactly sure what she'd expected, but I liked Julie already. She was real.

I heard talk of a folk dance that night at a school gymnasium in town. I think the idea came from Chris, master gardener, talented editor of *Talking Leaves*, and regional music aficionado. (He would prove a lasting influence on me, a role model even to this day.) I was disoriented and ambivalent, but decided to join the pile in one of the cars. We got to Eugene a half-hour later and I dissolved into the crowd, still in some culture shock. Two hours later I was drenched and loopy from do-si-do-ing with the locals. Spirits fairly soared on the ride home, and I found comfort and relief in the easy camaraderie.

It didn't last. Within a week I was hermetically sealing myself into my camper. I was struggling hard with something I could only identify as "spiritual correctness," a somewhat stifling community rectitude—and I took the only refuge I knew, solitude. The apprenticeship program called for extraordinary immersion in personal-growth practices of all kinds, and that alone would have tested me. But then, even the everyday protocols in the community, like greetings in passing, seemed suffused with an odd, reflective hyper-awareness, a heaviness I could hardly pinpoint, much less address.

Was it my lack of reverence? Should I have more respect, be more spiritual? Was it all in my head? Or was everyone just stilted and morose? I could not know, and it left a relatively hardened city boy like me questioning his marbles. In meetings, for example, custom called for avoidance of the word "but" for its negative energy, in favor of the word "and." I tried to flow with it, but I was clearly a square peg (I mean, "and" I was a square peg) in a round hole. I was craving an ease, a lightness of being, maybe even a dirty joke to make things feel more grounded, more real. And the more I struggled, the worse it got.

I went straight to the dictionary to confirm that she was indeed calling me an indolent, decadent, grape-eating faux-aristocrat.

My frustration, of course, aimed directly outward. In the morning sharing circle, I shifted and huffed while the other apprentices, who were roughly college-age and nearly all female, seemed only to want to process feelings—from last night's dramas to early childhood traumas. I was 30, male, and garden time was wasting. When my turn came it was always "Pass." In return for my hissing, judgmental bile, the women outvoted me nightly on the choice of kitchen-duty music (Ani Difranco—All-Ani, All-The-Time).

And so the tension mounted. At the weekly Well-Being meeting, I first encountered the process of "milling." Milling was where you drifted around a room from one person to the next, in a room full of people doing the same, stopping long enough to express aloud the single thought or feeling you would never otherwise want that person to hear. Then the other person got a turn, and then you moved on to the next one, and so on. The idea was, of course, noble: to foster deep honesty in a safe environment, to face difficult feelings from within and without, to grow and build a spiritual relationship with self, with other—with life!

I came up with a real humdinger of heartfelt communication: "You have a muscular back."

I wanted no part of it. I thought I did at first. But my virgin Well-Being had been torture, plain and simple. Conflicted and constipated, I faced one after another and croaked out some inanities that, mercifully, I don't remember. I finally got to one young woman, a fellow apprentice, and came up with a real humdinger of heartfelt communication: "You have a muscular back." I don't remember her reply, but it was downhill from there. Soon I was making myself scarce, same time every week.

Don't get me wrong. All told, the apprenticeship was a great success, in fact a dilettante's delight. I soaked up gardening wisdom at the foot of the master, Chris Roth; I learned (failed) to build a fire with sticks; I studied herbs and made candles; I stuffed myself giggly on roadside blackberries; I participated in powerful self-help seminars—taking my turn before 30 others to expand with loving, cosmic compassion one moment and to shudder in wracking grief the next; I swam naked in rivers and dodged rattlesnakes in the desert while fasting, alone, for three days—the mighty Vision Quest. And, ultimately, I was offered at least a provisional home at Lost Valley, if I so chose.

But between the high points, the doldrums always returned. I was always "almost-leaving." That poor community, I must have worn them out. But one day Dianne, a Lost Valley founder and elder, turned her infinite eyes on me during a meeting. She had the face (and spirit) of a shaman. She held both my hands and declared "I hope you stay." Not "good riddance" or "stop acting like an ass," but "I hope you stay." My momentum to escape broke then and there, and I finished the summer. She remains my dear friend.

By summer's end, the mood had lightened to the point where Larry and Karin, an important couple in the community, shocked a group of us at lunch with the hilarious, sexy, scandalous story of how they'd first met. I'd always liked them, but now I was getting the realness, the ease—the dirty joke—that I'd craved all summer. Only a couple of weeks earlier Larry and I had locked horns in a public, symbolic battle—a climax of tension between me and the community. Now as we laughed together I realized I could not blame "them" for my somber, often suffocating summer. I'd been the creator.

Lost Valley shaped my reveries so deeply that for years I wondered whether I should return there for the longer term. But the final analysis was clear: the Dilettante's adventures would continue.

MICK SOPKO

The field at Green Gulch Zen Center near Muir Woods, California.

Maplewood Farms

After Lost Valley, I learned not to be quite so dramatic with my search. A dilettante doesn't pull up all his roots and "change his life," sight unseen. To start with, he opts for smaller samples, and in that spirit, I arranged a night's stay with Maplewood Farms (not its real name), many hundreds of miles east of Lost Valley.

I love driving cross-country about once a year to visit my folks in Atlanta, so Maplewood was reasonably on the route. Also, I loved to read about Maplewood, more than about any other place. It just seemed too damned good to be true. They shared their income. They were stewards to hundreds of acres of wild forestland. They were numerous and, from the photographs, clearly happy. They played music in the woods and jumped off rocks into the river and ate together and worked harmoniously in any of a handful of bustling, impressive businesses. And this part of the country was stunningly beautiful. As the camper putt-putted over low, green, rolling hills, I could not wait to get there.

I hated it. I felt unwelcome from the first five minutes. They plugged me in immediately with the dinner crew, but for hours I chopped onions alone, failing to connect positively with anyone (I guess the newbie always gets onion duty). Some of the people were particularly ragged and, if not actually drunk, then two steps away. A woman brought a 12-pack of Budweiser to dinner and dropped it loudly on the front porch. The men vaguely glowered in my direction.

Aboard the SSCS vessel Farley Mowat.

The Dilettante was not accustomed to such treatment. The next morning I managed to gain the favorable attention of one lone angel, Mary Beth (not her real name), who introduced herself at breakfast and offered to give me a tour of the land. I almost wept in appreciation and relief. We walked and talked, around the pottery shed and through the cow pasture and down near the river. I was full of questions and she was ready to confide some inside scoops, certainly feeling some frustrations of her own.

It seemed Maplewood had been having a hard time keeping some residents in line—and keeping newcomers at all. They had a music and rec room, which I think they renamed the "wreck" room, since the evenings unfailingly ended in drunken brawling. In a vicious cycle, Maplewood became gun-shy from hosting a series of uninterested visitors—thus the cold reception for anyone not bubbling over to join the community, and thus more uninterested visitors. Mary Beth herself was struggling to extract herself from a troubled relationship with a young punk I certainly didn't like on sight. The feeling, I noticed, was mutual as we passed him on our walk.

I have no idea how Maplewood is doing now, a handful of years later. I never again visited their website or read their materials. I wish them well and take simple solace in knowing that I and, eventually, Mary Beth, both made our escapes.

I hated it. I felt unwelcome from the first five minutes.

Sea Shepherd Conservation Society

After a couple of years volunteering for environmental and political causes, I took a position as office manager with what I considered the purest, most bad-ass organization in the world: Sea Shepherd Conservation Society. Its founder Captain Paul Watson, at a mere 50, was a legend already. He has called Greenpeace (which he helped found but then disowned) "the Avon Ladies of the environmental movement," and he rams fishing and whaling ships at sea and sinks them in port, though without a single human injury and only if those poachers persist in violating international conservation law.

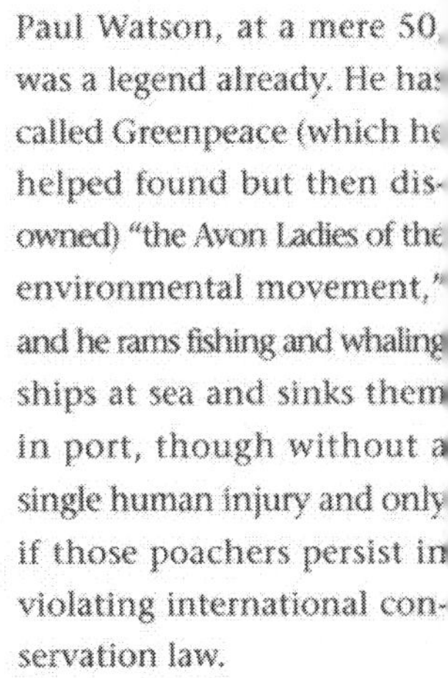

Watson is a controversial figure, as one might expect. I came to the organization admiring him but otherwise without any personal investment. The Dilettante, however, chafed in his job duties. Set up payroll? How on Earth does one do that? After six months of office managing I quit. I disliked the work, yes, but I positively loathed my direct supervisor (who was fired just two weeks after I quit). Nevertheless, in this role I had helped select about half the ship's current crew of volunteers, and I'd always wished to be one of them. So now, since I was unemployed anyway, I took the opportunity to sail aboard the *Farley Mowat* from San Diego up to Seattle as a Sea Shepherd volunteer.

I saw no combat on the voyage. I did wage one battle, though, against seasickness. I swooned and burped for days but never puked. (So did I win?) Anyway, even the salty crew admitted these were the worst seas they had seen all summer, and a few of them took to their beds for a spell. At night it was like trying to sleep on a giant roller coaster. I lay in my bunk for three nights, listening to the ship pop and crack and groan like a person, and wondered how the hell the thing stayed together. I considered a watery death and felt surprising serenity.

The crew could not have embraced me more warmly than they did, from the first night when they handed me a beer to the last waves good-bye as they putted and blared their way out of San Francisco Harbor. And they formed a perfectly harmonious, if unlikely, community. They had their strict assignments and carried them out as if in the military. Some had come on board only a few weeks ago and others hadn't left in years. The head mechanic was a crusty Brit in his early sixties. His assistant was a woman in her forties, soon to be the mother of an Iraq war veteran. A young woman from Germany, a conservatory-level musician, was 19. One gentle Canadian in his early 30s was a Disney animator. He drew hilarious, uncanny caricatures of the whole crew.

I disembarked in San Francisco, by the way, only because of the heavy seas. Seattle was another five days away, and I ain't stupid. But it saddened me to leave the Farley Mowat, and I could tell that a few crewmembers genuinely hoped I would change my mind. So to this day, the Dilettante will occasionally rub his chin and consider future whale-saving voyages with the Sea Shepherd "community."

Green Gulch Zen Center

Green Gulch is just too beautiful and good to be true. But there it sits anyway, successful for decades now as a Zen retreat center and sprawling seaside organic farm in Marin County, California. A stone's throw from the Golden Gate Bridge, towering eucalyptus trees line the steep hills surrounding their northern California land, which also neighbors Muir Woods, a jewel of the state's redwood preserves.

I, the Dilettante, am a spiritual seeker without a practice and an organic farmer without a farm. So, three springs ago, Green Gulch's six-month farm apprenticeship program was calling out to me. Apprentices participate fully in the community's formal Zen practice, as well as in the curriculum of the farm program. But before I could establish my candidacy, I had to complete a two-week trial run of meditation and work.

FRANK BEATY

SSCS crew member Joost Engelbert shows author Frank Beauty (right) the view from the crow's nest.

I am not sure if anyone ever really gets used to the impossibly loud, stabbing clang of a monk's hand-bell at 4 a.m. I can tell you that the Dilettante did not. However, for the first time in my life, I meditated in deep peace and comfort for two virtually uninterrupted hours, almost every morning. The Zendo at Green Gulch was the most serene and beautiful sanctuary I have ever seen. Giant globes hung low from the high vaulted ceiling, turned only to the dimmest setting in the pre-dawn. The quiet had substance, blanketing us and keeping us warm, and as the sun slowly took over and lit the windows high above the birds lifted the blanket, one chirp at a time.

For the first time in my life, I meditated in deep peace and comfort for two virtually uninterrupted hours, almost every morning.

This practice actually felt right. I could almost imagine a life here. But alas, I am a you-know-what, and so this two-week trial—a dilettante-detection device of sorts—discovered me and gently rooted me out. While other work-students at bedtime were reading Zen Mind, Beginner's Mind, I had hooked into The Party's Over—Oil, War and the Fate of Industrial Societies, and was freaking myself out but good. Also, I was chatting a lot with the farm apprentices and filling my notebook with names of nearby farms and farmers, stars from the world of sustainable agriculture. I started to chomp a bit at the bit.

I didn't leave Green Gulch because I was drowning in spiritual torpor. No, in fact I was delighted by the easy and down-to-earth, time-for-the-dishes kind of geist around the place. And I actually enjoyed the rigor. Green Gulch would emerge a clear and formidable contender for the Dilettante's affections, but I had only two weeks' vacation and suddenly much else to see. So after only half my scheduled stay, I set out on a one-week, whirlwind, seat-of-the-pants northern California sustainable-farm communities tour.

To be continued in the Winter '06 issue.

Frank Beaty works as a medical editor, volunteers in progressive politics, and is helping start both a community garden and an alternative fuel co-operative. As of this writing, he still lives in Los Angeles.

Author Frank Beaty, left, at Teaching Drum Outdoor School in Wisconsin.

The Dilettante's Journey, Part II

How do you pick a community to join if you're interested in . . . EVERYTHING?

BY FRANK BEATY

Author Frank Beaty considers himself a dilettante because he's "something of a dabbler, a sampler of life." In Part One he described his brief visits to Earthaven Ecovillage in North Carolina, Lost Valley Educational Center in Oregon, Maplewood Farms (not its real name), Green Gulch Zen Center in California, and his voyage aboard a shipboard community, the Farley Mowat, *as a volunteer for the Sea Shepherd Conservation Society. Never staying in one community long, the Dilettante next visited sustainable education centers in northern California.*

Occidental Arts and Ecology Center (OAEC)

I knew very little about Occidental Arts and Ecology Center (OAEC) except that reportedly the land was beautiful. It was the first stop on my spontaneous whirlwind northern California eco-community tour.

Redwoods, blue skies, the ocean just a few miles over the golden hills to the west, and crisp, technicolor brilliance form my lasting impressions of the area. OAEC's entire rural property seemed to rest on one hillside, so that its tilt was strangely uniform, and pockets of steeper slopes above hid clusters of yurts and cottages, barely visible behind lush foliage. As I started along the path, I felt a tingle. This place was enchanted.

The man who greeted me quietly in a French accent, Harold, offered to guide me to the gardens. We passed through a leafy archway of vines. Upon first glimpse of the first garden, I quite actually choked up. The Dilettante had sampled beauty in his day, but this field surpassed much of it.

Next I met Doug, head gardener and botanist, and his apprentices. As we worked and talked, my respect for Doug, for other residents I met at OAEC, and for the organization, took hold and deepened. The intentional community is called Sowing Circle; OAEC is its research and teaching foundation. Its last job posting, for example, called for someone to manage a water quality monitoring project for the region. Many of the OAEC staff are scientists as well as activists and communitarians, working in their region and nationwide to fight for environmental and related issues. On site, they teach courses in ecology, sustainable building, community, and art. Adam Wolport, a professional painter, directs OAEC's Arts Program and co-leads its course on starting new intentional communities.

Friday evening I attended the 2nd Annual Chautauqua show at OAEC's new outdoor amphitheater. This is a program based on the spirit of the Chautauqua movement that spread over the United States a century ago, which combined lecture, debate, entertainment, and practical education to benefit rural areas.

The audience of area locals murmured and filled the rich, polished hardwood benches. Community craftspeople had only recently built these benches into the earth, forming a permanent amphitheater under a twinkling grove of huge

OCCIDENTAL ARTS AND ECOLOGY CENTER

Community members, including Doug, the head gardener, at OAEC in California made quite a good impression on the author.

performances and engaging Native American bands. During a side-splitting piano revue that lampooned members of the community, I turned and found Doug in the audience when his name came up. I hardly recognized him; his quiet composure had dissolved into beet-red uncontrollable laughter. A woman brought a stool to the stage and delivered an eloquent update on the successful local fight against genetically modified foods.

As I started along the path, I felt a tingle. This place was enchanted.

oaks. A beautiful stage, also of hardwood, completed the circle and a stone-pit fire marked its center. Faerie lights strung in the trees filled the area with a glow. Before the show had even begun, I sat and basked in the feeling that this was my kind of place and these were my kind of people.

A fair young man opened the show playing a lullaby on tall, weird instrument made from an African gourd, which he had learned to play during his time in the Peace Corps in West Africa. He plucked the two dozen strings and sang perhaps the most heartbreaking song I have ever heard. After a moment of resistance I let the tears flow. No use fighting it.

After him, and separated by lively musical interludes, came mimes and hilarious skits and historical lectures re-enacted with poignancy and passion. I watched wild spoken-word

Every act was professional-grade, and the talent was all local. Afterwards, people visited friends they saw there or formed small groups at the fire for more singing and laughter.

The magic of the Chautauqua fulfilled every promise of the tingle I'd felt when I first came to OAEC, and it remains among my most cherished memories. I left reluctantly that night. And I still wonder how I might breach their ranks someday and return there, to fill a role and make a home. But theirs is a serious operation, and the Dilettante would have to raise his game a few notches before hoping to play with the big kids.

Ecology Action

Next I visited John Jeavons, the legendary gardener, author, and teacher of French-intensive, bio-intensive-style gardening at his farm, Ecology Action, near Willits, California. Jeavons shows you how to grow more vegetables than you ever thought possible, and on less land than you could ever imagine (and in fact wrote a book with a similar title). He started his tour with a classroom slideshow covering the history of human population growth, which took a slight dip during the Black Plague on its way to today's explosion. He told our group of visitors that the end of cheap hydrocarbon energy is upon us and that, at our present rate of soil erosion, thanks to today's methods of commercial agriculture, we have at best 40 years of topsoil left worldwide. At best.

In short, he scared the bejeezus out of us. His burly, grizzled presence added *gravitas* to his dire message. But he also soothed us with assurances that, with the proper techniques, we could grow enough food to feed a family of four, all in a small garden plot.

Next he led us down the terraced gardens of his farm. The flat land that holds Ecology Action's buildings abruptly ends at a cliff-side slope of 45 degrees. This steep hill is actually the growing area, and it looks out over the valley town of Willits, surely thousands of feet below. As you stand on the upper edge of this field, the effect is positively vertiginous, and I have never seen any farm so majestically severe. Cold springtime mist-clouds whip up this slope from the nearby Pacific, and dry August sun bakes the rocky soil. Often this farm endures these weather extremes in one day.

OCCIDENTAL ARTS ECOLOGY CENTER

The Dilettante was also mighty impressed with the show-stopping Chautauqua performance held in OAEC's outdoor amphitheater.

Most farmers would probably not buy this property, but here it is, flourishing. Jeavons has deep, sure knowledge of what works, knowledge borrowed from Middle-Ages Europe and gained from his own years of personal and staff research. You name the obstacle; he can overcome it. Hardship is his game.

Theirs is a serious operation. The Dilettante would have to raise his game a few notches.

He showed us the best way to compost, a method radically different from anything I'd learned elsewhere. He defined double-digging and demonstrated the most energy-efficient physical movements needed to do it. He urged the examination of exact calories burned growing a crop, versus calories yielded in that crop. He showed us cheap and easy ways to grow cash crops like lavender and prepare them for market. All his helpful hints rang with the knowing that tough times lie ahead for us all. But I didn't mind. I found his tone hopeful and his practical wisdom hugely valuable.

Ecology Action hosts a handful of well-educated, sincere interns from around the world, and my own tradition required that I consider, at least briefly, joining their ranks. But the cost of the internship was more than I could afford, and despite my deep respect for Jeavons and my keen interest in his approach, upon honest reckoning it became pretty clear that this weren't no place for no Dilettante.

Teaching Drum Outdoor School

In the summer of 2005 I was off again to visit intentional communities. I also set out to learn some basics of wilderness skills, of living on the land, Native-American style. I didn't necessarily want to live like that forever, but I hoped to find a viable community around such values and practices, and see where it might lead. Did such a place exist?

Teaching Drum Outdoor School hides deep in the North Woods of Wisconsin. The school offers a longer-term, more authentically Native American approach than your average Tom Brown-type primitive skills weekend course. Students at Teaching Drum, called "seekers," commit to a year-long course, living around a big national forest lake through all four seasons. In the warm months they learn tanning, fire-building, for-

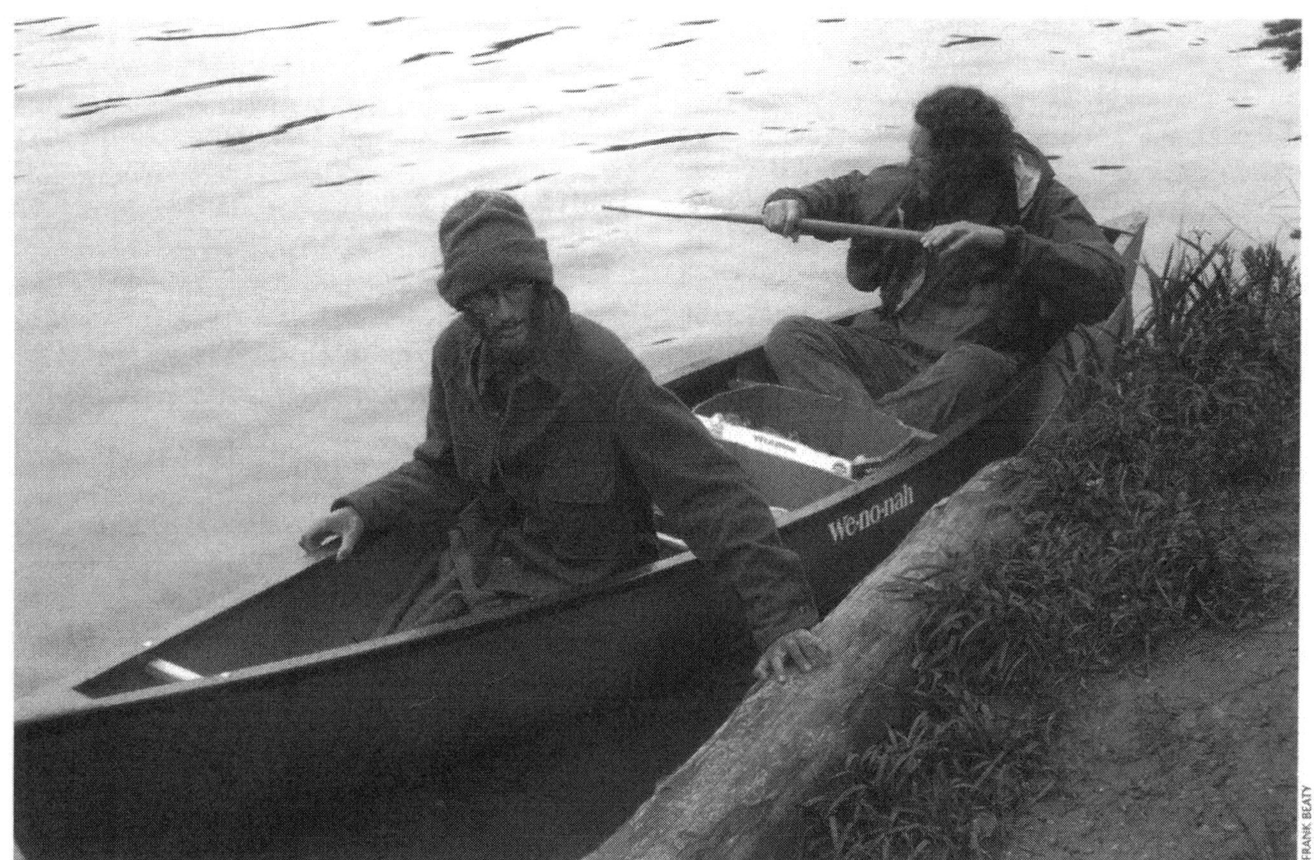

At Teaching Drum Outdoor School the author got introduced to the art of traveling by canoe.

aging for wild edibles, and Native purification ceremonies. In winter they learn to make snow-cave homes and then live in them. According to the founder, Tamarack Song, none of these skills will really live in you until you've learned to connect deeply with the land. That process takes time.

Tamarack had a huge gray beard and round specs, and he spoke softly, unblinking, as he greeted me. One of Tamarack's assistants, Glen, drove me from the school's cabins out to the lake where the students lived. We hiked through a rolling forest of birch and pine until we came to a primitive shelter in a clearing. We met a few students, then Glen canoed me across a wide, beautiful lake to meet my host camp, where we met more people, clad mostly in forest-green khaki. I bade Glen farewell and collapsed in my tent.

That evening another camp crossed the lake in canoes to join us for dinner. They brought eggs, wild greens, fruit, and some mystery meat, and combined it with our stashes to make a feast for a dozen. (The meat, I learned, was deer lung. Bright red when raw, brownish-gray when cooked, lung generally had to be fried to a crisp or else it was too chewy and spongy. It tasted like liver.) During dinner conversations flowed. People ranged in age from roughly 19 to 45, and even included a 12-year-old boy and his parents.

The instructors called meetings daily, all 25 or so gathering in a big circle under the birches. Here the casual conversations would meander from where best to harvest burdock to some deep personal or spiritual matter, long silences between topics and even between words. I spent the first half hour wondering "so when are we going to get down to the business at hand?" Eventually I realized this *was* the business at hand. The practical and the personal, instruction and inspiration, met and merged without transition. I began to see these meetings pulse and flow with the spirit of this, a very real community.

The casual conversations would meander from where best to harvest burdock to some deep personal or spiritual matter.

This crowd had personality and a keen wit. A student from Latvia, Alex, officially and repeatedly requested a class on eating bugs. He was maybe the skinniest guy I've ever met,

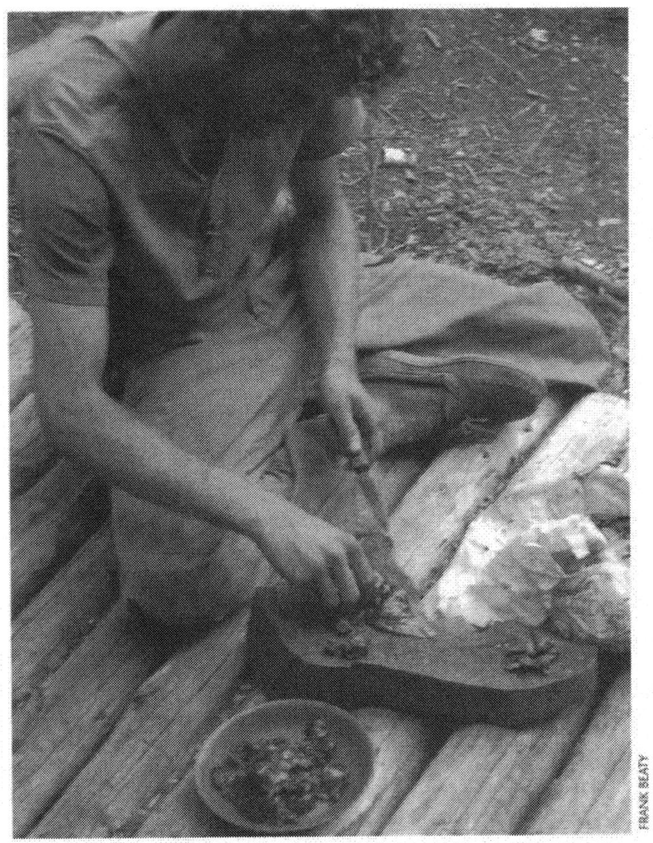

A Teaching Drum student prepares deer lung for the evening supper.

and was soulful and hilarious. The bug-eating class, despite his earnest consternation, had become a running community joke. I met young people, evolved and thoughtful, each of

Working feverishly and face-first in searing heat, I ran out of drinking water.

them on a quiet, profound quest for meaning. Some were anarchists, some poets. A few wore their depth (or damage) on their sleeves, while some had the light, urbane demeanor that I am more accustomed to on the "outside."

Another student, Matt, had appeared at the first meeting in a full buckskin suit he'd made himself, talking slowly through a toothpick about a fallen tree he'd found, in case anyone wanted to join him in a birch-bark harvest. Giving much credit to Teaching Drum, he told me later that he'd transformed himself from a belligerent, alcoholic, right-wing Navy sailor into the person I saw now: a man with clear eyes and a calm, even heroic competence. He liked to look far away into the forest, listening to things I could not hear, and then come back to me quickly with a twinkle and a teasing question.

Another student, Katy, single-handedly saved my ass on at least three occasions. When I'd first arrived and was searching forever and in vain for a tent site, Katy went searching herself, unnoticed. She returned presently, tugging at my sleeve, and led me to a perfect, level clearing. Late another afternoon, watching the skies, she suggested that we put a tarp over my tent, against my strong urge to stay near the fire and continue eating cashews. She worked like a mule on that tarp, with my feeble help, and got devoured by mosquitoes in the process. Throughout that night a vicious thunderstorm raged, but my tent stayed dry. I would have been a sopping, suicidal mess without her.

Days later I accepted the honor of serving as fire-tender for the sacred sweat-lodge ceremony. An insulated earthen dome became an oven as Tamarack led 20 naked students and teachers inside for a Native purification ceremony. That was their test; mine was to keep the huge fire outside blazing, while hauling massive, red-hot boulders from fire to lodge, one after another. Working feverishly and face-first in searing heat, I ran out of drinking water. But I was alone and couldn't abandon my post during the most serious ritual of the year. Just as my vision faded and I started to expire, Katy loped out from the forest like some mute angel, gallons of water in each hand. She'd served me and saved me repeatedly, automatically, with perfect timing, and without being asked. And not just for me—for everyone. It was simply her role: how she served, loved, and belonged.

During my short stay I learned some of the art and science of the canoe; I picked wild edibles for dinner; I learned to poop in nature and wipe with damp bog moss (the most difficult challenge of the week). I learned that mosquitoes will kill you if you let them—they'll just keep sucking, and call a thou-

Teaching Drum students found their deer lung dinner delicious.

sand friends over to suck, until you disappear in a terrible cloud and you have no blood left and you are dead.

I watched four young women take apart a road-killed deer with small knives, quietly and without complaint or hesitation. Over time they filled a box with neatly wrapped bundles of meat. The smell of guts hit me, and I watched the black-green flies swarm and bite. I found a leafy branch and shooed vicious flies from the women's exposed arms and faces. Allison sang a lovely song and conversations rose and fell, but this was difficult work, physically and emotionally. At least two of the women were vegan. One woman, Chelsea, went to bed before sundown, exhausted, and dreamed all night about the deer.

For three days the seekers fasted in preparation for the dreaded Mosquito Course. Tamarack declares mosquitoes the greatest teacher of his life. Naturally, he takes his students through the same kind of hell he's suffered. This course begins with a purifying sweat ceremony and culminates with the students venturing out to their own private forest spot, naked and still, and letting the satanic swarms have their way unhindered. Until I knew for sure whether I would participate, I fasted with the rest. Even after Tamarack and I decided that I would sit out the course (I ain't that stupid), I found very little

I watched four young women take apart a road-killed deer with small knives, quietly and without complaint or hesitation.

food. I ate three apples and a handful of Brazil nuts over my last two days.

I decided to leave after day five, and the goodbyes were sweet and true all around. But I confess I giggled like an idiot as I drove off, my heart already set on the first fried-chicken buffet I could find.

My time at Teaching Drum humbled me some. And no matter how madly the Dilettante dashed away from the place, I positively glowed with the discovery of yet another diamond out there, another priceless and precious community of people. For those people I hold nothing but love and gratitude.

Earthaven Ecovillage

Which brings me back to the remainder of my visit to Earthaven Ecovillage in North Carolina, in the spring of 2006. As evening came after a day of plucking roots from the Gateway Field agricultural project, I made my way to the Trading Post cafe for a snack and some wireless emails, courtesy of stream-

FRANK BEATY

Alex, a student from Latvia, officially and repeatedly requested a class on eating bugs.

fed hydro-power. Chris Farmer (called "Farmer"), the project's co-founder, came in, as he'd promised, to buy me a beer. His gratitude for my handful of volunteer hours at Gateway Field, I assured him, was excessive. But I accepted his kindness and raised my bottle in excited praise for the barn, the field, the whole damn thing.

Farmer's brother Derek had donated a full day out there too, and apparently he did so fairly often despite having plenty of work in Asheville. I had grown quite fond of his honesty and genuine kindness. As we wrapped up work earlier, Farmer had approached Derek and thanked him sweetly, adding that without his help they could never have finished the roof today. They hugged each other tight.

"You don't even know," Farmer told me over his beer. "My entire life, Derek has never raised his voice to me in anger. Not once. And growing up, even though he's four years older, every time I wanted to go with him and his friends somewhere, he always let me. Every time." All day I'd resonated with Farmer, with his co-founder Brian Love, with their commitment and vision to their Gateway agricultural project. And earlier, seeing Earthaven's land, learning about its projects, and meeting its people had excited and moved me just as much. But not until that moment, as I swigged my beer and looked around on the porch of the Trading Post, did I know I could make a life here.

But first things first.

I've scheduled a little talk with the Dilettante.

Frank Beaty works as a medical editor, volunteers in progressive politics, and is helping start both a community garden and an alternative fuel co-operative. As of this writing, he still lives in Los Angeles.

Interns and work exchangers learn a wide variety of sustainability and community living skills, like Volunteers For Peace volunteer Audrey Lothe, who learned to build with cob at O.U.R. Ecovillage in British Columbia.

What Interns and Work Exchangers Say *About Us...*

I absolutely loved my stay at Lost Valley, recalls Polly Robinson, who served as an intern and later a live-in course participant at Lost Valley Educational Center in Oregon. "I loved being surrounded by people of all ages who genuinely cared for me, and the generally relaxed atmosphere of the place, I felt like I was a community member the whole time I was there."

> ***"I went through a full-on transformation."***

Communities magazine asked a handful of temporary communitarians—work exchangers, interns, and live-in course participants—to share their experiences of temporary community. These women and men reported that their lessons were often planting and building; their teachers, the gardens, animals, and children.

Nathaniel Nordin-Tuininga, who also lived at Lost Valley, first as a work trader, then an intern, and lastly as a residential student, is equally enthusiastic about his time there.

"Interacting with Lost Valley and participating in both their permaculture and personal growth workshops taught me so much about myself, my relationship to the surrounding environment, and my connection ith others. I learned a great deal about my own capacity to ow and develop into the person I most want to be, while cul- vating a harmonious relationship to the rest of the natural orld. I was introduced to new ways of interacting with plants nd animals in order to meet my basic needs. I received per- onal instruction and hands-on training in land and garden ojects. I participated in yoga, dance, mediation, saunas, hot bs, stargazing, sports, games, group outings and other vents—and always had an amazing group of people to share ese experiences with. And emotional well-being was better ttended to at Lost Valley than in any other community I ave visited or been involved with."

Similarly, work exchanger Ron Laverdiere found true utopia t La'akea Community in Hawai'i, not because it was per- ect—but because it was real.

"At La'akea I was able to be fully honest with myself n all aspects," he reports. "This came from being trans- arent in relationships, offering support whenever it

"I learned to stretch myself."

vas needed and feeling supported at all times, plus the villingness of community members to connect in speech r dance or music."

Even the simple joy of eating food on the same day he helped arvest it amounted to a life-changing experience for him.

"Everything in my life was up for question and I resolved nany issues with the help of the community," he adds. "I vent through a full-on transformation during my time there."

Surprising perhaps is the amount of time such a transfor- nation required. In Ron's case—just a month.

As enthusiastic as many folks are about their time in com- nunity, some had concerns as well.

Nathaniel notes that finding enough personal space at Lost Valley was challenging at times.

Michael "Mojohito" Tchudi, an apprentice and then a vork trader at Emerald Earth community in northern Cal- fornia, found that the community's policies regarding nterpersonal interactions only served to become challenges themselves. "A disadvantage of maintaining a practice of nonconfrontational communication is that it was difficult and awkward to address issues of disrespectful or passive-aggressive behavior with permanent members of the community," he says.

Sometimes the short-term nature of the experience hindered the social acceptance of people who don't have an outgoing nature.

"As an introvert who doesn't make friends very quickly, I did sometimes miss the close relationships that long-term living situations have provided me in the past," recalls Carrie Dickerson, who lived at Twin Oaks Community in Virgnia for three months as a conference intern. "This was also my first experience living away from the city."

What's in a Name?

Work Exchanger, Work Trader. The community exchanges room and board for labor. Usually it's a straight-up trade, but sometimes the work exchanger pays a small fee; often just to cover the cost of their food.

Intern, Apprentice. The community offers a more formally organized educational experience with onsite courses and workshops as well as room and board, in exchange for labor and a substantial fee. An internship or apprenticeship is often in a specific area, such as garden intern, natural building apprentice, and so on.

Residential Student, Course Participant. The community (or one of its members) offers a formal educational program such as a class, weekend workshop, or longer-term course, and room and board, for a fee (and sometimes for work in the community as well). Community-based courses can include yoga, meditation, permaculture, natural building, herbal medicine, and so on.

—*Editor*

Polly Robinson

Michael "Mojohito" Tchudi

Molly Morgan

Mostly, however, the people we talked with found that their growth experiences in community far outweighed any challenges.

"Most notably I discovered that my capacity for physical work and exertion is far greater than I had thought, and that I am capable of working in rather extreme heat," observes Mojohito. "Maintaining a lifestyle of living close to the land and contributing in projects that directly benefitted both the community and myself was so satisfying."

Work trader Molly Morgan turned 50 during her three month stay at Emerald Earth, a milestone that she says was accidenta in timing but rich with its rewards.

"I learned to stretch myself while there," says Molly, whos interests were building and gardening. "I was learning so man new things, and I was really clumsy and slow at them, bu the community members were unfailingly supportive an patient with me. I learned that even at mid-life I could feel awk

What Community Hosts Should Know

"Be as transparent and up-front about expectations and opportunities as possible, such as, for example, different housing options available, and possibility for longer-term participation in the community," advises Michael "Mojohito" Tchudi, who served as an apprentice and work trader at Emerald Earth in California. "Also, permanent members need to be highly proactive in addressing internal issues and personality conflicts to minimize the negative effects these can cause on short-term residents," he cautions.

"Thoughtful planning, organization, and setting realistic expectations are key," advises Jodie Emmett, who has a background in nonprofit management and program development, and recently completed a 10-week natural building course in a rural ecovillage. "Expressing a realistic picture of the program will allow potential course participants to determine if it will be a good fit for them. Telling people the community is one thing but providing another underestimates the participants. This kind of dynamic requires the community to go above and beyond the students' expectations in order to succeed, but it usually just sets up the community for failure."

"The Emerald Earth people needed to interview me and also work with me to be sure they all thought I would fit in," recalls Molly Morgan, who was a work trader at Emerald Earth. "You can do a lot of interviewing, but there's always a vibe that's important to check out in person before you both commit to serious time together."

"Having a personal liaison or 'go-to' person from the community is helpful," suggests Travis Fowler, who was a work exchanger at La'akea in Hawaii. "Also, having an up-front agreement to how long a visit is going to last and/or how to deal with situations that aren't working out is very important. There shouldn't be any surprises surrounding this."

Ron Laverdiere, also a work exchanger at La'akea, found morning check-ins especially helpful. "Morning check-ins were a really good way of connecting community residents to each other," he recalls. "It also helped me to feel that I was important to the community. I had everyone's attention at least once every day."

—D.F.

ward and untalented and still be okay with learning new skills and processes. It was humbling and encouraging."

For many temporary residents it seems that the most amazing experience a community offered them was the simple gift of caring, a social blessing many reported to be far too rare in their regular lives in fast-paced, money-obsessed mainstream society.

"I loved the fact that the well-being of the people of the community was just as important as the work," says Polly Robinson about Lost Valley. "I loved that there was such a diversity of thought and ways of life, yet we all accepted each other, and for the most part, lived together in peace."

"I learned a great deal about my own capacity to grow and develop into the person I most want to be, while cultivating a harmonious relationship to the rest of the natural world," notes Nathaniel about Lost Valley.

Although the level of participation for temporary workers obviously varies from community to community, Molly recalls that Emerald Earth welcomed her into a role far more substantial than that of visitor or observer. She was made to feel just as welcome at the meeting places or around the kitchen table as any of the full-time residents.

"The community members were very open about their lives and inclusive of the work traders," she says. "There were very few meetings to which we were not invited. I asked a lot of questions and I was never once told it was inappropriate to ask that nor received any other bad vibe. This was especially important to me because the community was dealing with some very serious personnel issues while I was there and not knowing what was going on would have been very uncomfortable."

The problem occurs when participants see the gap between the founders' vision and what's actually on the ground.

She stressed that she'd never felt so well cared for her in life. "It was the first time I had ever had all my needs met—physical, emotional, social, spiritual. I had so much love and support that I felt like I was able to truly flourish."

Travis Fowler, another La'akea work exchanger, explained how living in such a radically nurturing environment truly proved to be the social garden he needed for growing into the person he desired to be in life. "I realized how emotionally closed I was in the 'real world,' how I could not express my true feelings or ask for what I wanted or needed for fear of being judged. The community was supportive and was a safe place to express myself. In the community, I felt more free to give the love I was keeping inside—and wow, that felt good!"

The communities in our small sample seemed to do a pretty good job making their short-term residents comfortable, too. Although rustic accommodations can often be a visitor's complaint, many of these visiting workers stressed that the drastic and unique change in housing and food only amounted to an even better experience for them.

"I felt particularly grateful to stay in a beautiful, hand-built natural straw bale and cob house," Mojohito says.

Travis Fowler

JAE STEINMAN

Guillermo Maciel.

JAE STEINMAN

Jodie Emmett

"I was always well fed, and always had a warm dry place to sleep, so my physical comfort along with everything else was well taken care of," says Polly about Lost Valley. (Yet Nathaniel must not have thought so, since he recommends "improved housing options during the rainy season" for the same community.)

Although Molly disliked her stint living in a tent at Emerald Earth, she raved about the meals. "The food—it was sensational! I ate a lot and still lost 15 pounds. It was great!"

"What I really enjoyed was the intense focus of learning natural building techniques, the opportunity to share our experience in the natural building trade, and the variety of people and experiences in the program," recalls Guillermo.

Yet the couple was surprised to find differences between their expectations of a course and the reality they found once they got there. For example, they expected to be living in an intentional community, but soon realized that only the program

Sometimes they didn't know what was expected of them in terms of work hours, community participation, financial arrangements, or how long they could stay.

Two short-term residents both liked and felt some disappointment in their community stay. Guillermo A. Maciel and Jodie Emmett were participants a ten-week natural building course at a rural ecovillage. "I liked the natural building teachers immensely," Jodie reports. "Two instructors in particular were incredible people; each was an inspiration to me. I also enjoyed the natural building projects we worked on in other locations, as well as the optional weekend workshops on specialized topics. Plus, we were living in a gorgeous setting."

TONY SIRNA

Ted Sterling

director/founder and his partner lived on the property on a permanent basis; the other founders either lived elsewhere or were no longer involved. "It would have been a lot easier for all of us if we were told in advance that there was no 'community' currently," Jodie observes. "And that the founding group was going through a transition and wanted natural buildings for what they would be doing sometime in the future."

Guillermo and Jodie also expected that they and the other students would have much more say in how they'd live their daily lives in a place which was billed as "your community." But they were often told that they couldn't do or make use of certain materials, go to certain locations or use certain buildings on the property, or employ certain kinds of communication styles. "It was difficult to tell when appropriate regulation of behavior was for the common good of our 'community' of students, and when it was just micro-managing us to fit the program director's vision of community," recalls Guillermo. It gradually became clear that there were three distinct parties on the property with different rights and responsibilities: the program director and his partner (resident owners who had final say on everything), the program staff (who reported to the program director), and the course participants, who didn't in fact have much decision-making voice. "There was a genuine intention to create an inclusive environment and avoid an 'us versus them' mentality," he adds, "but unfortunately, towards the end of the program, we failed in this intention." The process was exacerbated when the program director would change the rules about what was expected of participants, or what was or was not allowed on the property. It would have helped, Jodie points out, if there had been complete transparency about the role the students were to play in the evolution of the ecovillage.

Yet the couple respects the program director and admires what he's trying to accomplish in the project. They don't believe he misled the group consciously. "I think the idea that the community belonged to everyone is part of his vision about what a community could and should be, and he was trying to tell this to *himself*—like having his own personal mantra," Jodie speculates. "I don't think he could be honest with himself about the real situation, because visionaries can live inside their visions—the problem occurs when participants see the gap between the founders' vision and what's actually on the ground."

In fact, the most common concern of the people *Communities* interviewed was "structure." Many of these temporary residents, while insisting on the magic of their stay, admitted that the lack of a more formal structure ended up cheating their experiences out of some of the potential worth. They gave examples of not knowing what was expected of them in terms of work hours or community participation, a lack of communication regarding financial arrangements or how long they could stay, and sometimes a general lack of any kind of direction for the work they were expected to do.

Several suggested that communities who host short-term workers designate a go-between who could meet with them not just as the beginning of their stay, but several times throughout the visit to check their progress.

One suggested that communities also work to get a commitment from long-term residents in terms of their treatment and involvement with visitors. "Make sure there is a solid commitment on the part of as many community members as possible for including temporary members and rolling them into the fabric of daily life," advises Ted Sterling, who served as a three-month intern at Dancing Rabbit Ecovillage in Missouri.

But Ted certainly liked what he saw at Dancing Rabbit, so much so that a year and a half later he moved back and remains as a full-time resident today.

"I met my partner here. We now live here in a home we built and have had a child together, Aurelia, who is not quite six months old," he says. "Talk about life changing! I consider myself a changed person."✪

Darin Fenger works as a newspaper reporter in southern Arizona.

Planning Your Own Community Adventure?

Field-Tested Advice from Interns and Work Exchangers

If you're planning your own short-term stay in community, consider the advice of these experienced community visitors.

• Get comfortable with the community members. I was hesitant to open up at the beginning, but when I saw community members speaking from their hearts, it made me comfortable enough to follow suit. Do your research. I read about La'akea first, and went there with some confidence that I would fit in. It's important to know what you're getting into. *—Ron Laverdiere*

• Don't be shy or embarrassed to ask questions or ask for what you need. Strive to be emotionally honest—even if what you have to say is not the 'easy' or 'pretty' answer. Don't be afraid to share affection or appreciation. Be confident that you can handle anything that comes your way. *—Travis Fowler*

• If you have a good sense of what you want to learn and experience while at a community, make sure you communicate what you want clearly and have an agreement about how this is going to happen. Go into the situation with an open mind and heart to see if you can learn and experience things you'd never have imagined. *—Molly Morgan*

• Discover and establish boundaries between your personal time and community time. If you don't take the time for personal space, it may become difficult to engage fully with the community. Keep an open mind, actively seek out projects that engage you, and cultivate kindness. *—Michael "Mojohito" Tchudi*

• Live it fully. Plunge in with abandon and trust those around you to respond to your zeal. Act as a community member to the extent that you can, contributing to making the community one that you would like to live in. *—Ted Sterling*

• Ask yourself ahead of time how participating in the community's program is part of your own vision and values, and how it will further your own goals. *—Guillermo A. Maciel*

• Even if you already know a lot about community or the subject of focus in its course or program, really learn to be a student; stay in a proactive observer space. Take what you need from the experience. And if things aren't quite what you expected, know that you can change your experience; it's only temporary! *— Jodie Emmett*

—D.F.

Wilderness Journeys Meet Cooperative Culture: Teens in Community on the Trail

By Mary Murphy

"I think we should decide this by consensus," Albert declares, running a hand through his wild uncombed curls. Eight teens and two adult guides are circled up on a flat spot on this steep mountain trail in New Hampshire. Our bulky backpacks are lined up on the side of the trail, and everyone is sipping water from their colorful Nalgene bottles.

"Okay, who's going to facilitate?" Eric asks.

"I will! Let me get out some paper to keep stack," Rita volunteers. "What is the question again?" she asks, swatting at a mosquito that buzzes around her head.

"We need to decide whether we are stopping for the night at the campsite that's closer, or pushing on to the one that's still four miles away," I remind her. "Our decision needs to fit with the Leave No Trace guidelines we have learned, so we have to stay at an established campsite."

The group settles down on the ground and dives into the consensus process. Albert, ever the organized thinker, points out that the longer we hike today, the less distance we'll have to cover tomorrow when we traverse the Presidential Ridge. Bobby grimaces at his words, rubs his sore calves, and reminds the group how nice it would be to stop early today and make a really nice dinner and play some games. Rita scribbles notes and stack lists on her writing pad, biting her tongue with concentration as she tries to keep up with the lively discussion.

This group knows each other well: we have just finished a nine-day canoe trip in Maine and this is our first day on the backpacking section of this wilderness trip. As in any community, there is a wide diversity of strengths, weaknesses, and personal styles among these teenagers. Some are very fit and eager for a challenge, others are out of shape and want to drag their feet. Some think of the group first, others feel a need to prioritize their own needs. I'm lucky to work as an expedition guide for Farm & Wilderness Summer Camp, a Quaker-based camp that already embraces many of the principles of consensus in its daily routine and culture. On this trip my co-leader (who was trained in Formal Consensus in the student co-ops at Oberlin College) has taught a simple consensus decision-making process to our trip group. She and I have facilitated it for them twice before, but this is the first time the campers have done

A musical canoe journey on the St. Croix River in Maine.

Pauliina Tuominen

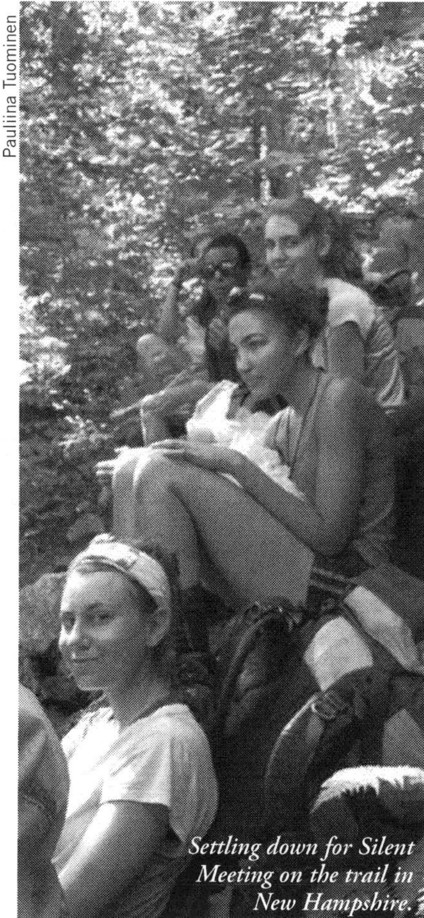
Settling down for Silent Meeting on the trail in New Hampshire.

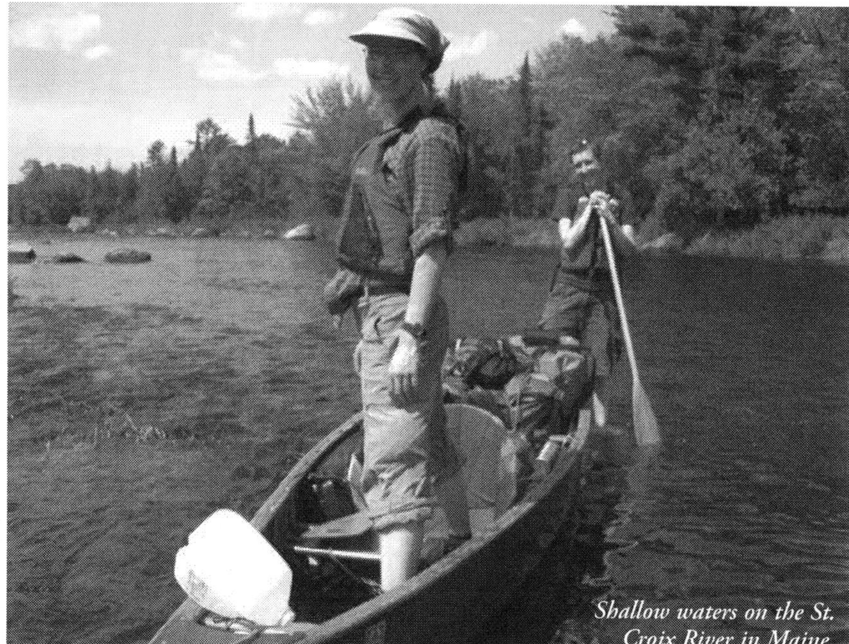
Shallow waters on the St. Croix River in Maine.

Photos courtesy of Mary Murphy

the whole thing on their own.

The discussion grows and weaves in the dappled shade of the mountain birches. Finally Rita announces a series of proposals and the campers all vote. Three pass, and a new discussion blooms about how to best combine them into one decision. The end result is a complex and nuanced negotiated agreement that involves dinner recipes, the time we get up in the morning, who has to retrieve the bear-hang food stash for breakfast the next day, and promises to play a round of the game Mafia on top of Mount Washington when we get there. I never would have guessed all these things were pertinent to a decision about where to camp for the night, but the glow on the teens' faces show me that they were. They are all relieved to have navigated the consensus process successfully, and they shoulder their backpacks with an enthusiasm and determination that never would have surfaced if I'd made the decision for them.

I've been leading wilderness trips professionally for eight years, and following the intentional communities movement for 12 years. While I find that many wilderness guides I've worked with don't know what an intentional community is, the culture of the outdoor education industry embraces many of the same guiding principles as communitarians do. A wilderness trip group is its own community, albeit a temporary one. Each trip has a different synthesis of individual personalities, so wilderness guides have to learn to set up community structures and norms that will accommodate whoever shows up. Unlike most residential communities, we can't screen out members of our trip community based on emotional maturity or willingness to compromise. Whoever pays the trip fee will come on the trip. Therefore, most wilderness guides who last more than a year or two in the profession are those who learn to nurture harmony and cooperation amidst the many kinds of diversity they find on their trips. We use many of the same strategies residential communities do: creating shared agreements, rotation of leadership, fostering trust, sharing emotions honestly, and mediating conflict.

I have found that many kids take to this like a fish to water. After they are taught the skills and see them modeled a few times, they start initiating these techniques themselves. In the opening scene of this article, the teens themselves decided they could use consensus to make the decision. Having seen it work well twice before, they suggested it immediately when the conversation about campsites began to feel tense. Kids instinctively recognize healthy cultural norms when they experience them,

Working as a team to portage canoes and gear around a dam on the Androscoggin River in Maine.

and they naturally gravitate toward them. While many adults come to this work with emotional scars and triggers from the past trauma of living in a hierarchical power-over culture, kids have less emotional armor and an incredible willingness to try new things. The level of functional community that a group of teens from diverse backgrounds can create on a 15-day wilderness trip rivals that of any intentional community I've visited. The number of lifetime friendships that are forged on my trips attests to the staying power of positive group culture.

So, let's learn from the youth! Below is a list of some of the group-building activities and conflict management strategies I use on my wilderness trips. All of these are teen-approved and have worked well to foster a community culture among the youth I work with. Most of them are common activities that are used widely across the outdoor education industry.

- **The Group Agreement:** The night before the trip starts, the group gathers together and brainstorms guidelines, behaviors, attitudes, and norms that they would like the group to strive for on the trip (always phrased in the positive). The agreements typically include respectful communication, positive attitude, following safety guidelines, using forest-friendly Leave No Trace practices, etc. We talk about what these statements mean to each person, discuss and clarify any controversial ones, and, once everyone can agree, we all sign the agreement. We carry this agreement with us on the trip and refer to it whenever conflict arises. In essence, this is a simplified version of the agreements and bylaws most intentional communities create for themselves.
- **Fears in a Hat:** On the first night of the trip, we sit in a circle. Each person writes down three fears they have about the trip and we put all the anonymous slips of paper in a hat. We each draw out someone else's fears and read them aloud. Typically many people share common fears, so hearing that others have the same worries eases their minds. This also helps group members take actions to prevent triggering other group members' fears: if three people said they are afraid they won't be able to keep up, the speed demons in the group may be inspired to self-regulate their pace (and the guide can remind them of the fears when addressing impatience).
- **Truth Circle:** In the evening we sit in a circle, speak a self-reflective question or prompt, and then pass a talking stick. Each person may talk for as long as they

Teens celebrating their new confidence on the Presidential Ridge in New Hampshire.

Portaging a canoe in the backwoods of Maine.

like with no interruption. The talking stick goes around the circle again and again until no one has anything else they'd like to say. In this way we learn how others think about themselves and have a space to speak vulnerably in a safe and predictable environment.

- **Evaluation Circles:** Every few days we circle up and each person answers two questions: What do you think the group is doing well? What do you think could be improved? We speak our answers and promptly move on to the next activity. This activity fosters awareness of group dynamics and how behaviors are affecting others, while also asking each person to think about what is working for the group, not just what is working for themselves. The evaluation circle acts as a self-correction mechanism for the group: usually everyone takes action to improve dysfunctional dynamics that have been spoken in the circle, without any discussion or nagging.
- **Leader of the Day:** Every day a different camper leads the group. They carry the map and compass, they decide when we have rest breaks and where we have lunch. This mirrors the systems of non-hierarchical leadership that inspire many intentional communities to rotate their leadership roles.
- **Silent Meeting:** When working for Farm & Wilderness, a Quaker-based camp, we have a daily 20 minute gathering to sit in silence together in a beautiful spot. This shared reflection time allows our spiritual selves to be honored in the same place without any layers of dogma. I find that the shared silence brings the spirits of all the trip participants into a quiet harmony once a day, gives us a break from any conflict that may be present, and fosters an attitude of gratitude. Many spiritual New Age communities open their meetings with a period of shared silence for the same reason.

I hope these activities will inspire readers to try some new strategies for keeping their own communities cooperative and dynamic, and offer kids who don't live in community a way to learn about cooperative culture: go take a hike with a wilderness guide! ❧

Mary Murphy is a community-minded wilderness guide. After eight years of guiding for teens, she has recently started her own wilderness trip company (www.mountainsongexpeditions.com) focusing on spiritually grounded backpacking and canoeing trips for adults and families. She lives in Worcester, Vermont, on a cooperative homestead she shares with four adults, two kids, and various goats, chickens, and llamas.

A hazy mountain view in the White Mountains of New Hampshire.

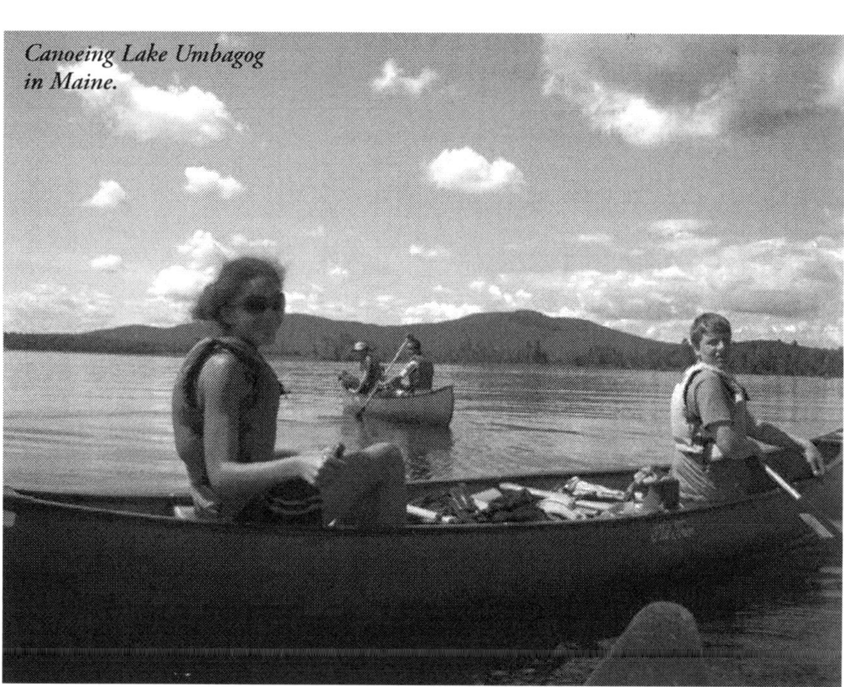

Canoeing Lake Umbagog in Maine.

A Mental Health Patient Seeks **(But Does Not Find)** Religious Community

By John Wachter

As a mental health patient seeking an alternative to mainstream treatment, I've looked to various religious intentional communities for better solutions. Over a number of years, I have spent at least a couple weeks apiece at over a dozen different residential religious centers, from varying traditions (Buddhist mostly, but also yoga and Catholic).

I first became seriously interested in religion because I developed a serious mental illness. In addition to being severely depressed about the fact that I had been having auditory hallucinations for the past two years (although they had nearly ceased by then), I was very paranoid when I first came to an intentional community. I had also developed an unhealthy preoccupation or obsession with psychic and paranormal phenomena and a substance abuse issue as well. I did not feel comfortable talking about being crazy and I didn't feel I had to, although I regretted that decision later. I spent five months at a lay religious center and it helped me feel much better, although I never formed any close relationships and left without any real answers to my questions about reality. I had come to the conclusion that the correct path for me to follow would be a religious life, so my next stop was at a monastery, where I spent a month, which caused me to rethink my path again.

Over the next three years I visited many religious communities, contacted many more, and struggled with my mental health issues. I had no friends other than my family during this time. I never found a place that seemed to support me. They told me what they wanted me to do, but not *how* I should deal with the things that prevented me from doing it. Failure was met not with understanding and encouragement to do better, but with impatience and anger. When I left the community no one ever referred me to someplace else that might be a better fit for me or followed up to check on how I was. (At best, I'd be put on a mailing list, but the communication was never personal.)

I understand that every community has leadership or authority of some kind and I accept that. It was always the methods that were difficult for me to accept. My first complaint is that I didn't feel cooperation was wanted, but only obedience. It was their way or the highway. Discussions rarely happened, but preaching was consistent. And when they were talking about or trying to instruct their way, it never seemed to be honest and frank, but instead cryptic hints and no accountability.

I obeyed all the rules, but I still felt very unworthy, unwanted, and unwelcome.

Many times there was also a quantity of hypocrisy. A lot of lip service was given to ideals that seemed to be absent. People in these communities didn't seem to be any wiser or happier than people in the secular world. If these communities are supposed to be places of healing, the people need to work on their bedside manner. One last thing: I always felt guilty because I couldn't afford to give much money to the community, I had (still do) a difficult time holding a job. Most of the programs are rather expensive.

I got very angry at the end of these three years and finally was hospitalized and entered the mental health system, which, in retrospect, I should have done much earlier. During the next six years I stayed away from the communities, although I would stop in with local centers on occasion. Unfortunately, I failed to build a life for myself in society, so I once again turned my attention back to the community scene. I revisited the first of the communities I had stayed at because they had been helpful, and some new ones, once again got turned down by many more, including the monastery I had spent a month at, but found living in community even more difficult than when I was younger. Despite the fact that I was obeying all the rules and informed them of my mental health past and present, I still felt very unworthy, unwanted, and unwelcome. I never stayed for more than a few days because I'd get too angry and depressed. Fight/Flight response perhaps. I thought it would be better to leave than stay and say or do something that I'd regret, since I found the intensity of these emotions overwhelming.

I have always been stubborn, and slow to understand implied wishes, I prefer people to be direct and frank with me. So, I guess I should've given up earlier. I had just studied so much of the literature and wanted so much to do what was best, that I couldn't give up, even when it was obvious the advice in the books wasn't working. Not to mention that I've never been successful at much of anything in mainstream society, anyhow.

Finally, I wish to express gratitude to the Abbey of the Genesee for so clearly and definitively informing me that someone who has had such a history of emotional and mental issues would find living in their community too difficult. The unambiguous answer was welcome. I just wish I had heard it three years ago when I started looking at religious communities again, instead of rejections without explanations, or a group allowing me to visit but not caring whether the visit was a good one or not. I'm considering looking for a non-religious intentional community, but not sure that it will be much different.

John Wachter is a 33-year-old American who lives in Arizona. He has been on mental health disability for many years.

Nashira: An Ecovillage from the Grassroots

By Giovanni Ciarlo

Attending the Llamado De La Montaña (Call of the Mountain) Bioregional Gathering in Atlantida Ecovillage in Colombia this last January, and witnessing the emergence of the new Latin American organization, C.A.S.A. (Consejo de Asentamientos Sustentables de las Americas), was one of the most enriching and energizing experiences I've had in recent times. And although I really wanted to visit other Colombian ecovillage projects while I was there, I had time to see only one, Nashira, an urban ecovillage near the Colombian city of Cali.

Nashira, which means "Love Song" in the ancient local language, was one of the most amazing ecovillages I have ever visited. It is run by low-income women heads of households. This reflects a widespread social problem in the outskirts of cities in Colombia, where decades of civil conflict has left many women to manage and sustain the household. A Nashira pamphlet states *"The Nashira project goes beyond offering just housing solutions, it seeks to provide a better quality of life, offering a secure and nutritious supply of food within the compound, an environmentally friendly atmosphere, and a source of income through the development of workshops where women can manufacture their own products."*

I arrived in Nashira just before sunset. I was introduced to some of the residents and shown to a unit where I had a reservation to spend the night. I was met by Osiris, the 30-year-old son of Marta, the head of the house. As a sign of the changes undergone by ecovillage members, Osiris is a social sciences faculty member at one of Colombia's rural Universities, and was visiting his mom for the holidays, something I thought was itself out-of-the-ordinary for people in the lower-income social class. He showed me to my room, a spacious, well-lit single bedroom on the second floor of the 700-900 square foot home that Marta had helped to build during one of the training sessions offered by national and international ecovillage consultants.

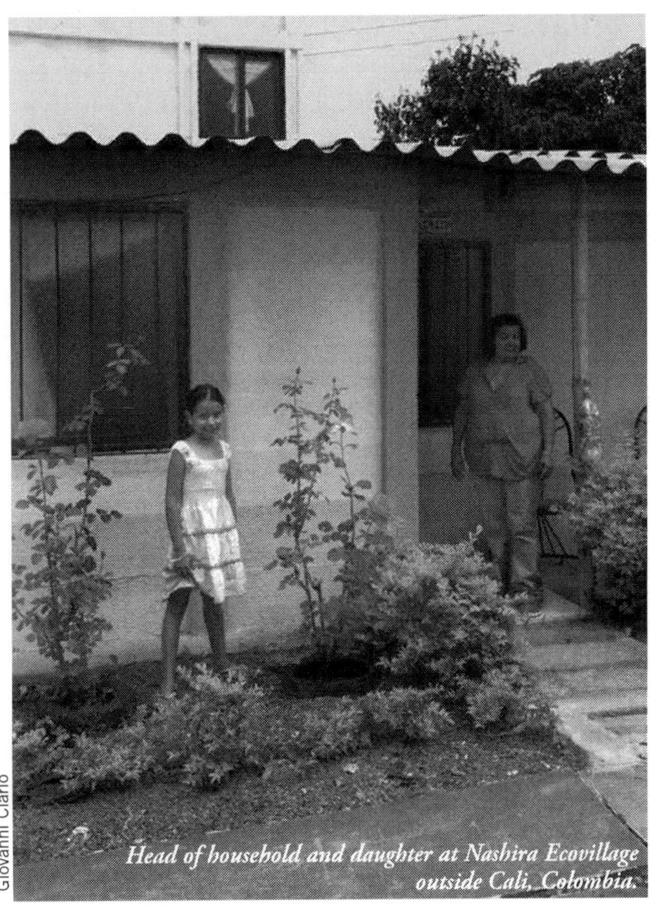

Giovanni Ciarlo

Head of household and daughter at Nashira Ecovillage outside Cali, Colombia.

I hurried to meet Osiris outside for the last bit of daylight to give me a flash tour of the ecovillage. Nashira was founded by a donor who gave the municipal authorities 30 hectares of land to build an 88-home ecological development for women heads of households with matching donations from government housing development funds. To date 48 units are already built, mostly with the sweat equity of their owners, who formed cooperative groups to learn and help each other to build small, attached, efficient, and durable housing units with the assistance of some additional materials, donations, and capacity training. Both national and international organizations spent time teaching ecovillage design and hands-on skills, from village economics (including small businesses that can operate from inside the village) to food production, decision making for self-governance, natural building, bed-and-breakfast ecotourism, a local solidarity economy, alternative renewable energy technologies, and waste management for recycling and recovering of industrial byproducts. One of the organizations doing the trainings is Change the World, where several ecovillage activists in both GEN and ENA work to bring low tech solutions to indigenous and marginalized people and natural reserves in Latin America. Among them is Beatriz Arjona, one of the organizers of the Llamado de la Montaña event and a member of Aldea Feliz, another ecovillage active in RENACE Colombia—the Colombian ecovillage network, now C.A.S.A. Colombia.

Osiris showed me the common house, a remodeled pre-existing farmhouse where now there is a computer lab and community center. Across from the common house is the solar restaurant, where one can find pastries and coffee during the weekends, and during special events there are cookouts using solar reflectors to grill, boil, fry, or bake many different local dishes with food grown on site. A dirt drive path passes the communal dry toilet built with bottles, mud, and bales of hay. It is beautiful, with the air of a temple or a pagoda where one would go meditate. Art is everywhere, complemented by well designed landscaping that takes advantage of the location to create gardens and paths around the site.

The shallow pool that children play in during the hot sunny days of the tropics is equipped with a converted bicycle pumping mechanism that is instructive as well as functional—pumping water from the well below to fill the pool and to create a waterfall from about eight feet up a wooden tower. The sound is soothing and children use it as a play station while they shower and enjoy the water and the sun.

We were able to see a number of housing units, and greeted people as they came outdoors to wave at us in the last minutes of dusk before dark. Osiris explained how there are several window-stores in some of the houses that sell snacks and beverages as well as some fresh and canned goods and cooking supplies. He told me that people form cooperatives to have more buying and selling choices. He showed me the partridge egg co-op, the chicken co-op, the cassava processing co-op, the recycling and restoring center, the children's daycare, and the rest of the land.

I was blown away at the achievements of this adventurous group of women. They all came from very disadvantaged sectors of the urban population. Most of them lived in shantytowns and cardboard shacks before getting the opportunity to apply and be selected for the project, creating an ecological community of similar women from the grassroots and poorest families in the Cali region.

Nashira impressed me because it is the first example I have seen of an ecological community, aligned with values promoted by GEN, which has emerged from the bottom up. It is a response and a solution to the housing and poverty issues of the oppressed, in a country that has seen decades of civil strife and violence affecting the majority of people, especially those living in the lower economic rungs. It was created not by a population from the privileged sector of society but by the poor, uneducated, economically distraught women leaders with families and dependents of all ages. Added to this mix was the right combination of aide and guidance of national and international agents, alongside committed activists and individuals empowered to help people from the oppressed sector improve their livelihood, because they believe it is possible and it should be done.

Before going to bed I spent time chatting with Marta, Osiris, and Natalia, his younger sister, about growing up in this village, and the opportunities ahead for them. They were upbeat and positive all the way. Natalia is also about to start college, where she hopes to study architecture so she can help others build affordable sustainable housing. The next day I took a refreshing cold shower, and as part of the cost for staying overnight, received a hefty breakfast of partridge eggs and toast followed by fresh brewed coffee. They even arranged calling a taxi to take me to the airport in the early hours of the morning. That's what I call *"Hospitalidad Latina."*

Seeing Nashira was like taking a breath of fresh air in the middle of the wilderness. It has given me renewed hope for a new society, that I like to refer to as *the reinvention of everything*, from our worldviews to the way we govern ourselves, the way we relate to Mother Earth, and the way we create local cooperative businesses that aim to provide right livelihoods to community members.

Giovanni Ciarlo cofounded Huehuecoyotl Ecovillage in Tepoztlán, Mexico in 1982. He is a Board member of Global Ecovillage Network (GEN) and is active in Gaia Education as developer of ecovillage design and education materials. He traveled to Colombia as council representative of ENA (The Ecovillage Network of the Americas). He also performs Latin music in the United States and Mexico with his group Sirius Coyote. Contact him at giovanni@ecovillage.org.

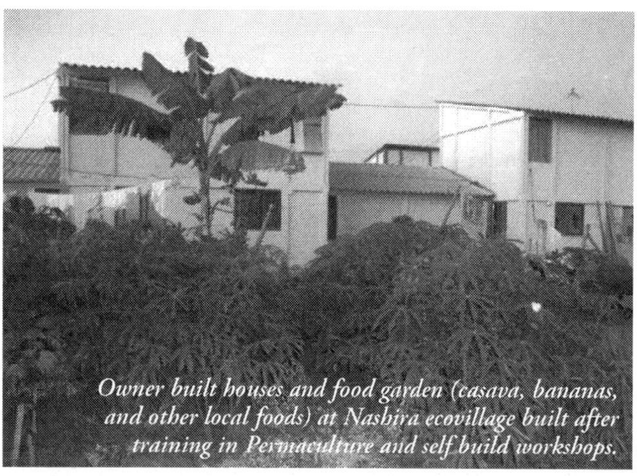

Owner built houses and food garden (casava, bananas, and other local foods) at Nashira ecovillage built after training in Permaculture and self build workshops.

The ENA and CASA group in ecovillage Atlantida, Colombia.

Ecovillage Radio

By Russ Purvis

What do Zegg Ecovillage (Germany), EcoVillage at Ithaca (upstate New York), Los Angeles Eco-Village (southern California), and Konohona Community Ecovillage (Japan) have in common? Perhaps you would be surprised at the common threads which run through all of these intentional communities, that also like to be known as ecovillages. Their common philosophical threads form the ecovillage "glue" for the periodic internet radio shows that have now been broadcasting since 2008, attracting over 11,000 listeners worldwide. Not exactly a viral sensation, but it is reassuring to know that on all the continents excepting Antarctica we are not alone. Ecovillages and the culture that pervades them are everywhere!

Many of us arrive at our destination in a roundabout way. It was no different with the birth of Ecovillage Radio. I had been fascinated with intentional community and the concept of an ecovillage for many years, and had helped create some shared living houses. After visiting artists' communes and reading about other living experiments like The Farm (Tennessee), I got to visit a serious ecovillage in 1995, Findhorn (Scotland). I haven't been the same since.

As I climbed deeper into the alternative living experiment I became a founder of Kakwa Ecovillage in British Columbia. During these years of observing and interacting with many members and potential members at Kakwa, as well as ecovillages around the world, I began to wonder about this organization called GEN—Global Ecovillage Network. They seemed to have a lot of great ideas and incredible people, but no apparent marketing strategy.

Since I now was part of the ecovillage family and daily breathed as well as bled "ecovillage," I was open to new ideas that might advance the movement. I discovered the relatively new medium of internet radio in 2008 and a start-up company called BlogTalk Radio. I knew nothing about radio, interviews, or how to get started, but I knew lots of people in the ecovillage movement and many were keen to contribute to the programme. It is no different today, with the exception that my skills have improved, and BlogTalk Radio now charges a fee to a host for an extended show. In the early days it was all free, as long as you had a decent internet connection and a separate telephone line.

The programme has evolved over time. What has become amazingly obvious is the fascination with the founders and members of ecovillages, which dominate the many shows we archive online at Ecovillage Radio (www.blogtalkradio.com/ecovillage-radio). We also explore other ideas relative to sustainable living strategies from time to time, such as formal Ecovillage Design, education for sustainability, and how to grow various crops. Imagine 40 minutes devoted to growing and storage of potatoes, with an expert grower of 30 years! Sometimes we encounter edgy moments like the "Who's your Daddy?" question while interviewing a member of ZEGG (known for the sexual openness of its culture), or the cat policy at EcoVillage at Ithaca. Seems the cat policy was evolving, but the knowledge of a parasite that cats can carry and its potential hazard to human fetuses was not a light-hearted subject.

Recognizing that nothing can take the place of an in-person visit or vacation experienced in an ecovillage, nonetheless it can be pretty juicy to visit a variety of ecovillages, countries, and their cultures virtually, through the eyes of a founder or long-term member. That has been the primary focus of Ecovillage Radio. We answer some standard questions you might pose about their land, infrastructure, housing, degree of income sharing (if any), pet policy, money required to join, etc. We also provide the opportunity to share about member demographics, and most importantly any unique aspects of the community.

For those who might be curious about the monetization of Ecovillage Radio and similar efforts, I have to report the "bad" news. It's basically a labor of love. The current internet radio broadcast opportunities do not provide much advertising revenue for the host in the beginning. However, the digital world moves so quickly that this may have already changed by the time you are reading this article.

Russ Purvis, M.Sc. is a founding member of Kakwa Ecovillage Cooperative, British Columbia, Canada (www.kakwaecovillage.com); a Council member of ENA—Ecovillage Network of the Americas; currently President of the Ecovillage Network of Canada; and Host of Ecovillage Radio.

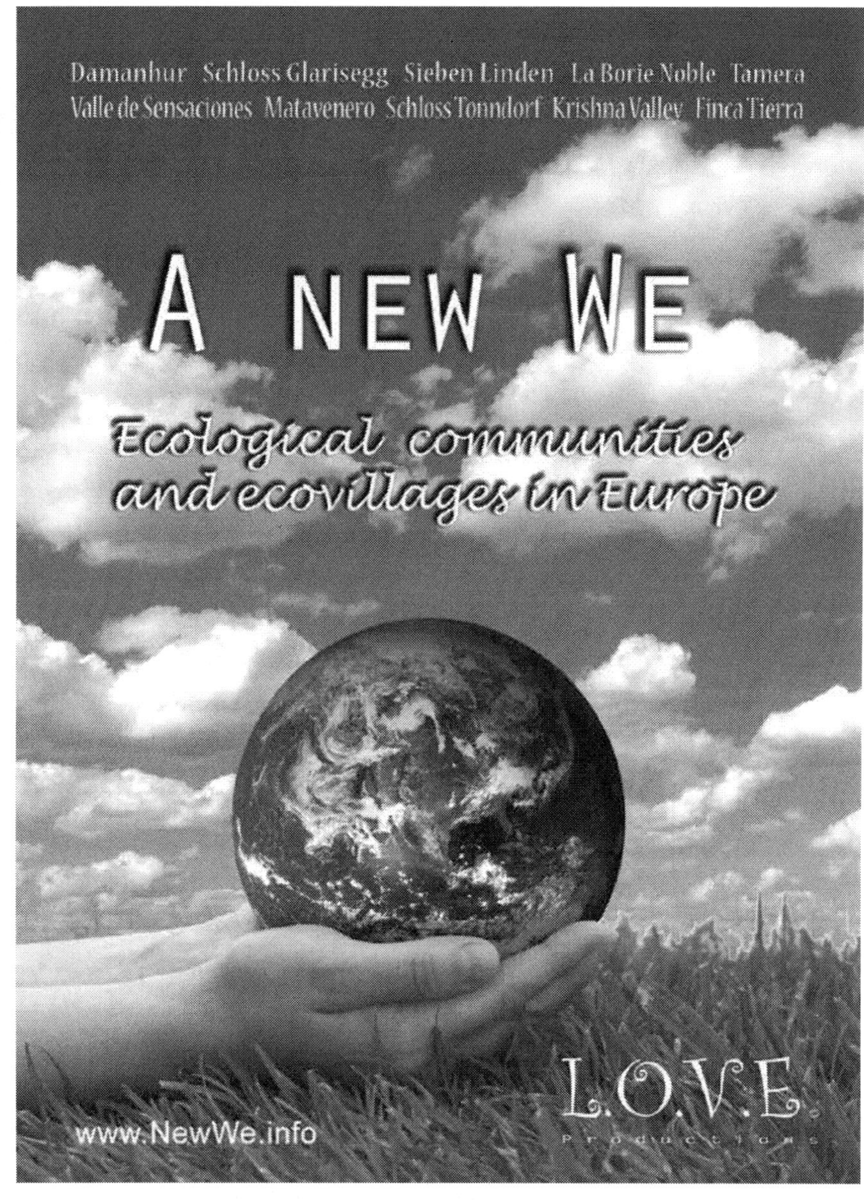

Damanhur Schloss Glarisegg Sieben Linden La Borie Noble Tamera
Valle de Sensaciones Matavenero Schloss Tonndorf Krishna Valley Finca Tierra
A NEW WE
Ecological communities and ecovillages in Europe
www.NewWe.info
L.O.V.E.
Productions

Hopeful New Stories from the Old World

A New We
Ecological communities and ecovillages in Europe
DVD, 120 minutes, L.O.V.E. Productions, 2010
www.NewWe.info; fic.ic.org/a-new-we.php
Available from store.ic.org/a-new-we

Two hours does not seem like a lot of time to visit even one community, let alone nearly a dozen. Yet Austrian filmmaker Stefan Wolf has managed to accomplish something amazing: he has created a feature-length film that gives viewers a sense of real familiarity with 10 diverse ecological communities and ecovillages throughout Europe. Even more important, by profiling such a wide variety of communities, all of them mold-breaking experiments in ecological living and cooperation, *A New We* leaves one with the feeling that the possibilities for such projects are endless. Stefan reminds us that these 10 are just a small subset of thousands of like-spirited experiments worldwide (a glance at the Communities Directory or visit to www.ic.org backs up his assertion), but his film also makes clear that nothing is "cookie-cutter" about these groups—quite the opposite.

Against a backdrop of beautiful videography, each community segment starts with a concise textual profile of the group (including number of residents, land area, organizational structure, percentage of diet produced on site, energy and water sources, etc.) and ends with contact information. In between, we visit each place and hear from some of its residents. The pace is never rushed, and yet each segment covers a wide range of topics, including some of the personal challenges that community members face.

The video tour includes: Damanhur, an Italian network of 1000 people living in 20- to 30-person eco-communities; Schloss Glarisegg, a 34-member Swiss holistic seminar center; La Borie Noble, a 13-member community in France inspired by Gandhian ideals of nonviolence; Krishna Valley, a 150-member Hungarian community with 95 percent food self-sufficiency; Matavenero, whose 70 residents inhabit a formerly abandoned Spanish mountain village rebuilt through the Rainbow movement; Schloss Tonndorf, a 60-resident, especially child-friendly German ecovillage encompassing an old castle; Finca Tierra, a small, nature-based community in the Canary Islands; Sieben Linden, a growing 120-member German ecovillage with a radically reduced ecological footprint and innovative decision-making model; Valle de Sensaciones, a remote Spanish

(continued on p. 79)

HOPEFUL NEW STORIES FROM THE OLD WORLD

(continued from p. 80)

eco-community emphasizing direct experience in nature; and Tamera, a peace education and research center in south Portugal inhabited by 200 people.

While Stefan obviously chose interviewees who believed in each project (rather than seeking out, for example, disillusioned ex-members, of which I would guess there are some), the candid nature of the interviews here make each video portrait both believable and ultimately inspiring. I never felt as if I were being "sold" anything, only given a window into each way of life—one that effectively conveys how hopeful and game-changing these kinds of life choices could be as humanity faces an uncertain future.

Of course, in reality, a 10- to 20-minute video portrait can only scratch the surface of what there is to learn about each group. I sensed that there were many more stories to tell about each place, which a video of this length could never hope to include. Based on my own community experiences, I could sense (or project) unspoken dynamics and issues into several of the settings. I never found myself rolling my eyes, but I did raise my eyebrows at the opening of one segment, in which the female cofounder is peddling away on a human-powered washing machine while her male partner lounges in a hot-tub and philosophizes about luxuriating in the senses. (Later, though, this comically unbalanced first impression is corrected when he introduces us to an intriguing mandala game he designed to distribute household tasks in a fair and fun way.) In another segment, I couldn't help but wonder about the power dynamics in a small community created by a single visionary individual; and in another, about whether members might eventually backtrack on their current degree of buy-in to a shared spiritual philosophy, and whether there were any "doubters" that we didn't meet.

But none of these questions derailed the experience of watching the video; instead, they just provoked more curiosity. I found myself interested in learning more about every situation.

This English-language edition of the original foreign-language film includes overdubs and, where more appropriate, subtitles—done, mostly, with skill, and always understandable.

A New We could not have come at a better time. It can benefit both current communitarians/ecovillagers and those who don't yet even know that eco-communities exist. It opens our eyes to the amazing diversity of approaches to eco-community that are possible—and even more important, to the fact that those dreams are being put into practice by real people, in real life, at various places all over the globe. ❧

Chris Roth (editor@ic.org) edits Communities.

CREATING COOPERATIVE CULTURE REVIEW BY CHRIS ROTH

Cycling toward Sustainable Community

Within Reach

By Mandy Creighton, Ryan Mlynarczyk, and friends
Into the Fire/Reach Within/Doctrine Productions, 2012, 1:38 run time
DVD available from withinreachmovie.com

Nearly five years in the making, *Within Reach* is a major new documentary about the promise of intentional community and cooperative living. Its creators suggest that the dream of "sustainable community" is within reach of all of us, and, through their personal story, offer many possible paths to that hopeful future.

Mandy and Ryan left their mainstream jobs and lifestyles to cycle 6,500 miles across the United States over a period of two years, visiting 100 communities of many different flavors and talking to people everywhere they went about ways of living more sustainably. Accompanied at times by fellow videographers and additional cyclists, they documented their journey, assisted by a crowdfunding campaign. The monumental task of wading through, excerpting, and editing together portions of their countless hours of footage into a coherent film took another couple years.

Happily, the result is a broadly-appealing mixture of "road trip" movie, community documentary, and exploration into practical approaches to social and ecological sustainability. Entertaining and understandable enough for a mainstream audience, it also delves deep into the "sustainable community" movement to offer fresh material to even the most experienced communitarians and eco-living activists.

Its central conclusion is perhaps best summed up by cohousing pioneer Jim Leach: "Community is the secret ingredient in sustainability." In scene after scene, we see vibrant pockets of community, and witness firsthand all the ways in which cooperation allows and encourages people to live more lightly on the earth while creating resilient webs of mutual support.

Eight years after doing service work together in Central America, where they first experienced "small communities living simply, in harmony with nature," Mandy and Ryan (who fell into much more conventional, increasingly unsatisfying lives in the interim) find each other again and decide they want to recapture the magic they felt there. They embark on an epic "quest for utopia," hoping eventually to find a new home aligned with their ideals.

The film documenting their journey ingeniously overlaps several thematic progressions. Its structure is not entirely linear, but rather a set of overlaid patterns. While most of the visits are presented in chronological order, this is not a rigid guideline; when it serves the purpose of the movie to jump ahead or back to a setting or interviewee with something important to say about a theme, it does.

One progression (indicated by three dimensional letters embedded in the landscape at the start of each new section) attempts to answer the initial question, *what is sustainable community?* The answers, in order, are that community is sharing; community is family; community is a legacy; community is food; community is education; community is service; and community is economical. The film then poses and attempts to answer another question—*what does it take to live in sustainable community?*—and concludes with suggestions about creating community wherever you are.

Another progression concerns type of community. We start with cooperative houses, then visit cohousing groups, transition towns, ecovillages, spiritual communities, extended communities growing "beyond the community border," working

(continued on p. 78)

WITHIN REACH DVD REVIEW

(continued from p. 80)

farm communities, groups focused on education and self-education, service-oriented communities, and a green town.

While we see relatively short clips of dozens of different communities, certain groups get significant segments of at least several minutes each; these include Earthaven, The Farm, Cobb Hill, Ecovillage at Ithaca, The Possibility Alliance, Dancing Rabbit, Joyful Path, Hummingbird, and the "green town" of Greensburg, Kansas.

The film also catalogs a broad range of sustainable-community-related practices and technologies (often highlighted with on-screen text), including consensus process, solar cookers, suburban farm animals, community kitchens, skillshare workshops, gardening and permaculture, natural building, community potlucks, eating local diets, "unschooling," homemade entertainment, neighborly collaboration, and eco-retrofitting.

Our view alternates between the small picture—one couple's trip around the country—and the big picture—national and global social and environmental trends that make a change of direction toward "sustainable community" paramount for our survival. Richard Heinberg, Bill McKibben, Rob Hopkins, Aron Heinz, and others offer valuable insights, interlaced throughout the film, on everything from the end of cheap fossil fuel, the urgency of addressing climate change, and the increasing dissatisfaction and social isolation in America over the last 50 years, to the importance of localization, of deep listening, and of self-examination. Just as valuable are the reflections of community members on what life in community is like for them. While they tout its many benefits, they also discuss some of the challenges: decision-making can be an ordeal, and compromising can be difficult. As one Cobb Hill resident observes, our culture doesn't teach most of us how to live in community, so we have a steep learning curve when we decide to.

Fortunately, community can also be an ideal place to safely engage in the emotional and inner work that helps us become better community members. That work is necessary to create the "social sustainability" that, many in this film observe, is the backbone of ecological sustainability. "The way we treat the planet is really connected to how we treat [each other and] ourselves," says one student visiting Ecovillage at Ithaca.

Yet the magic of community is felt most directly not through words, but through the many scenes in which community members are fully engaged in creating "sustainable culture" themselves—through sharing music, food, play, practical projects, helping one another live not only more ecologically but more joyfully. The spirit of community is palpable, leaving viewers with the (correct) impression that there is a whole world of cultural and ecological-living innovation awaiting them, if they move beyond the constraints of mainstream America.

An engaging soundtrack—comprised of homespun music reinforcing the grassroots perspective of the film, alternating with interviews, the bikers' reflections, and community scenes—helps the movie stay stimulating and dynamic. The videography, surprisingly professional given the sometimes challenging traveling and shooting conditions, conveys the experience of the journey well. Titles and captions are also used to excellent effect.

My favorite single segment depicts the Superhero Alliance in La Plata, Missouri—probably the most radical experiment included here, a service-oriented group operating on the gift economy and dedicated to simple living not dependent on modern technology. In this section, the power of engaging in "emotional inner work" is perhaps most clearly described: speaking in candlelight in this electricity-free community, with flashes of lightning visible through the windows behind her, Keren Ram describes how healing it is for people to "see my dark areas and still love me" in an environment that is so supportive and embracing of each person's humanness. She also conveys clearly the power of shared dedication to being present and spiritually centered, of which the "bell of mindfulness" is a common reminder at the Superhero Alliance Sanctuary.

(I must admit that my personal acquaintance and several longstanding friendships with those we meet in this segment help make it my favorite. In fact, the movie is full of people I know and/or have at least met, part of the extended community network of friends and colleagues that helps this feel like a "movement" rather than just a set of of isolated cultural aberrations.)

The magic of community is felt most directly through the many scenes in which community members are creating "sustainable culture" themselves.

Every in-depth segment has its memorable moments and revelations, from the interviews with the children participating in Ecovillage at Ithaca's Primitive Pursuits program (best line, from an extremely imaginative child: "It's not imagination!") to the reflections from ex-suburbanites learning rural skills at Cobb Hill and from ecovillagers learning how to create homes for themselves at Dancing Rabbit.

For someone already familiar with much of the intentional community landscape—and perhaps for any viewer—the most inspiring, hopeful segment may be the depiction of Greensburg, Kansas. Following a 2007 tornado that destroyed 95 percent of the town, townspeople banded together to rebuild using green principles, doing community planning as a group. They decided not to re-erect their backyard fences, but instead to encourage neighborly interaction wherever they could, while adhering to an ecological approach that, rather than being dogmatic, meets each person "where they are" and helps them move organically toward more sustainable practices.

Greensburg's mayor, Bob Dixon, is one of the most eloquent voices for community in this film. Describing the social isolation that has overtaken our society in recent decades, he says it's time to change from being "back porch, back patio people," walled off from one another, into once again being "front porch people," who get to know our neighbors and thus are able to deal much better with the issues we'll inevitably face together. Perhaps because they've learned the lessons of the tornado, the town's residents all seem up to the challenge of working together. The fact that such a radical movement toward sustainability and community can happen in a "regular" middle American town inspires real hope that it can happen anywhere.

Each town, city, or rural area may need to confront its own form of "disaster" in order to make such a transition. Since current trends suggest that we will have no shortage of those in coming years and decades, the best we can hope for is that we start making these changes before the full force of disaster strikes. In an age of resource depletion and climate change, such an approach can mitigate both local and global suffering.

At one hour and 38 minutes, this film cannot be exhaustive in addressing the issues it raises, or in depicting all dimensions of the intentional community world. One fundamental question that it does not answer is: are any of these "sustainable communities" truly sustainable? They are all clearly moving in the direction of, or working towards, a way of being that is regenerative rather than self-destructive—but in the modern world, true "sustainability" is hard to ascertain and may be impossible to achieve without larger-scale, more fundamental changes. Even Mandy and Ryan's human-powered trip around the country was fueled by many "unsustainable" elements. The idea that simply by moving to (or creating) a place calling itself a "sustainable community" we've achieved sustainability strikes me as an illusion. Instead, all any of us can do is take steps toward what that kind of world could be; it seems unlikely that any of us will arrive there in this lifetime.

The movie does a good job of depicting both the joys and challenges of Mandy and Ryan's bike journey, including mechanical, breakdowns, injuries, difficult weather, dwindling finances, hostile authorities, and personal and relationship challenges (at one point, we learn, Ryan has smashed his computer and quit the project in frustration—he later apologizes, relents, and rejoins Mandy). But it doesn't maintain the same balance in its depiction of the communities the couple visits.

True, as already mentioned, multiple interviewees talk about some of the difficulties they've experienced; especially in the areas of collective decision-making and compromising our personal desires, they remind us that our culture hasn't taught us how to live in community. But we viewers don't see these difficulties first-hand. We don't experience any of the pain and disappointment, the frustrations and breakdowns of various sorts, that happen in community just as they happen on bike trips. In effect, with each community, we—like the short-term visitors we're accompanying—are in a "honeymoon phase." We get to see how appealing each place can be; we don't get to feel how challenging it can be. And ironically, when interviewees talk about the challenges, their honesty makes their communities seem even more appealing.

The most common criticism of this film is likely to be that, while it opens viewers' eyes (including mainstream viewers' eyes) to many new horizons related to sustainability and community, it does so through rose-colored biking glasses.

However, one movie cannot be all things to all people. This one is a surprisingly in-depth introduction to the wide-ranging world of forward-looking community-building. It demonstrates that it is possible to leave a mainstream lifestyle and enter into a world that most people only dream about. It also shows that one can make changes in one's own life and community to move much closer to a future that is healthy and friendly to both people and the planet. The film doesn't hit us—at least not viscerally—with the potentially discouraging news that life in community can be just as challenging as life outside of it, fraught with potential pitfalls. However, if we are making conscious choices, these pitfalls occur in the context of a reality we feel more aligned with, and that has more staying power than the lives we've left behind.

The movie concludes with Mandy and Ryan's arrival at Hummingbird, the community they have chosen as their new home—"but," an on-screen caption tells us, "their journey toward a sustainable life never ends." In the years since their bike trip ended, they have in fact moved on from Hummingbird. Mandy now lives at Dancing Rabbit, and Ryan, having tried Dancing Rabbit as well, now lives outside of intentional community, in Hawaii. In other words, for each of them (as for anyone who commits to an extended exploration of community), the "honeymoon phase" has passed.

Yet the lessons of their film remain just as valuable, and the journey they share is a compelling one. This documentary deserves to be seen not only by those in the "sustainable community" movement, but by a much larger mainstream audience as well. It has the capacity to change lives—and, whether creating ripples or waves, it can make a real contribution to the more regenerative, community-based future that, we hope, is still "within reach." ❧

Chris Roth (editor@ic.org) edits Communities.

Made in the USA
Columbia, SC
11 November 2021